ABOUT THE AUTHOR

Richard H. Buskirk, Ph.D., is the H. Lay Professor of Marketing at Southern Methodist University and the author or coauthor of six other books on business and marketing.

Dr. Buskirk's interest in Machiavelli began early in life, and, as he read more of the philosopher's work, he became convinced that Machiavelli's reputation of "deception, unscrupulous cunning, and dishonesty" was unwarranted. With this book he hopes to stimulate a general reassessment of Machiavelli's philosophy and a recognition of its validity and utility for the modern manager.

A graduate of Indiana University with a Ph.D. from the University of Washington, Dr. Buskirk has also been Professor of Marketing and Chairman at California State University and Professor of Marketing at the University of Colorado. He is a member of the American Marketing Association and the Academy of Management.

Modern
Management
and
Machiavelli

Modern Management and Machiavelli

RICHARD H. BUSKIRK

CAHNERS BOOKS
A Division of Cahners Publishing Company, Inc.
89 Franklin Street, Boston, Massachusetts 02110

54400

Library of Congress Cataloging in Publication Data

Buskirk, Richard Hobart, 1927–
  Machiavelli and twentieth century management.

  1. Management. 2. Machiavelli, Niccolò, 1469–1527.
I. Title.
HD38.B84   658.4   74-11194
ISBN 0-8436-0734-3

Library of Congress Catalog Card Number: 74-11194

ISBN: 0-8436-0734-3

Printed in the United States of America
The Book Press, Battleboro, Vermont

Designed by Richard Kaseler

Contents

THE DISCOURSES:
FIRST BOOK

Contents

THE DISCOURSES:
SECOND BOOK

THE DISCOURSES:
THIRD BOOK

Contents

Preface

Sometime during my school days a teacher remarked that I "exhibited strong Machiavellian tendencies." Not knowing whether I was being praised or damned, but suspecting the latter for the former was a rarity, I scurried to the library to learn of what I had been accused. The dictionary proclaimed:

1. of, like, or befitting Machiavelli: *Machiavellian astuteness*.
2. being or acting in accordance with the principles of government analyzed in Machiavelli's

The Prince, in which politicial expediency is placed
above morality and the use of craft and deceit to
maintain the authority and carry out the policies of a
ruler is described.

3. characterized by subtle or unscrupulous cunning,
   deception,   or   dishonesty: He   resorted   to
   Machiavellian tactics in order to get ahead.
4. a follower of the principles analyzed or described in
   The Prince, esp. with reference to techniques of
   political manipulation.

As I was contemplating giving the teacher's house a bit of
special attention come Halloween, I wondered what in the
world was in The Prince that I was following. And so I came to
know Niccolò Machiavelli and I was perplexed. I could not see a
relationship between the bulk of his advice and the reputation
of "deception, unscrupulous cunning, and dishonesty" that he
had achieved. Most of his advice seemed rather sensible—a
matter of common sense; to do otherwise seemed stupid.

Niccolò advised the Prince to avoid threatening either the
property or the women of the populace. Yes, that might disturb
the teacher, for she had custody of most of my worldly
possessions—water gun, et al.

As the years evaporate, my wonderment at people's perceptions of Machiavelli grows. A few years ago, the editor of a
campus newspaper took me to task for having the brazen
academic affrontery to have my students read The Prince and
then write a paper applying Machiavelli's thoughts to the job of
the modern manager. It did not seem fit for students to read
such things according to his line of reasoning. "Ah, yes," I
thought. "There is nothing so liberalizing as a good general
education. And here we have on display its results—the
editor." I looked him up to see if he had any inkling of what he
was talking about.

"Have you read Machiavelli?" I inquired.

"No, and I don't intend to."

"Why not?"

"It's evil, the bible of the degenerate capitalistic warmongers."

I left the room. Conversing with parrots has never held much attraction for me. But I reflected, wasn't he rather typical—"putting down" a work in ignorance based on the stereotypes passed down through the years, mindlessly, by those either too lazy or too naïve to make the effort to understand what Machiavelli really said.

I submit a *prima facie* case: Any book written in 1513 that has survived the evaluation of all the intervening generations must have considerable merit or else it would have perished as have most of the literary works from that era. Moreover, I suggest that Machiavelli's basic advice is not only applicable to the ruling of a state but is also germane to the problems of managing any organization.

Thus I have set forth to do three things. First, I think it wise to present Machiavelli's actual words in context, not my rewording of his thoughts, so the reader can make his own interpretations. One caution—many times Machiavelli says in essence "If you *must* do such and such, then here is how you should do it." In such cases, he is not recommending an action—in fact, many times he strongly advises against an action, citing the probable adverse outcomes—but is merely accommodating the ruler in power by advising his conduct in an action that is a foregone conclusion.

Second, I have edited from *The Prince* and *The Discourses* material not relevant to the management of men. I saw little point in pondering whether artillery is superior to infantry. Moreover, I have italicized the key sentences that present the essence of Machiavelli's proposition.

Finally, I have inserted my own comments after some italicized passages, illustrating how they apply to modern management. At times I take the opportunity to expand Machiavelli's thoughts and there are instances where I disagree with him.

Please realize that Machiavelli does not offer a total or even systematic treatment of management but rather merely makes some observations on various matters he felt were important to a leader who wanted to maintain his position or to someone who aspired to leadership. Many important aspects of the administrator's job are ignored. I do not try to fill in the voids for I think that most inappropriate for this work. Rather I am only trying to take what Machiavelli wrote and apply it to some modern managerial settings. I did not feel it appropriate to try to offer other writers' views on the same topics, thus providing a more balanced treatment of the subjects.

I want to thank Dr. Earl Goddard, Dean of the School of Business at Oregon State University, for his patient and painstaking work with me on the manuscript. He was of great help.

Special thanks are deserved by my editor, Mike Hamilton, who saw sufficient merit in this work to make it a reality.

As usual, I cannot give too much credit and thanks to my most able assistant, Sylvia Arnot of Boulder, Colorado, for her fine efforts.

RICHARD H. BUSKIRK
Dallas, Texas
June 1974

The Prince

Of Hereditary Monarchies

I WILL not here speak of republics, having already treated of them fully in another place. I will deal only with monarchies, and will discuss how the various kinds described above can be governed and maintained. *In the first place, the difficulty of maintaining hereditary states accustomed to a reigning family is far less than in new monarchies; for it is sufficient not to transgress ancestral usages, and to adapt one's self to unforeseen circumstances; in this way such a prince, if of ordinary assiduity, will always be able to maintain his position, unless some very exceptional and excessive force deprives him of it; and even if he be thus deprived, on the slightest mis-chance happening to the new occupier, he will be able to regain it.*

Roy, who had been highly successful selling for a large food products corporation, was unhappy with his seemingly slow advancement into higher managerial echelons. He had been a product manager for five years when the owner of a small but fast-stepping food specialty processor lured him away to be general manager with hints that one day, if all went well, he could not only be head man but also could own a piece of the action.

Roy did a great job—sales and profits rose significantly. Yes, the old man had a son, but that was not news. The lad seemed so hopeless that he could not possibly manage the business. Unfortunately he did not know he was hopeless and his father would not admit it, at least openly. Perhaps he hoped that his son would grow into a man if forced to assume responsibility. Whatever, Junior came into the business and was soon made boss over Roy.

The kid took over. Daily operations became confused as he compounded his mistakes with errors. He took an order over the phone one day and then forgot to write it up; when he remembered it, he sent the wrong goods to the wrong address. He would tell an employee to do something and then bawl him out for doing it when the action proved to be in error. He let work pile up on his desk and would not answer his mail. Sales dropped and cash became a problem as the lad invested in such necessary business equipment as a corporate yacht.

Roy was doing his job and waiting to be called to the helm to save the ship. But this simply wasn't going to happen. The father would not dethrone his heir: "He is my son. He'll shape up. Give him time." The old man really just could not bring himself to let control of the enterprise out of his hands, and nothing the minority stockholders or the old, faithful employees said could change his mind. His son would be given every chance to "grow into the job."

And need you be told who the kid blamed for the decline and fall of his empire? At last report, Roy was still trying to find a "new connection."

Admittedly it's an old story, but wishful thinking seems to blind some people to the fact that family businesses are different than publicly owned ones. The family's welfare comes first, and members of the family will usually be preferred over outsiders. Moreover, the family will protect its less talented members.

Interestingly, hard-nosed businessmen refuse to hire friends or relatives. Bob Teller, owner of a highly successful chain of fast food outlets, put it nicely: "It's all a matter of the differences in expectations. When you hire a relative, or a friend, or a relative of a friend, he expects that you won't expect as much of him as you would of a stranger, and you expect more of him because of the connection. So he expects to do less work, while you expect him to do more. Therefore, it's not likely to work out."

Hereditary monarchies come in many forms, and they can prove most tenacious even though horribly incompetent. There seems to be some deep-seated desire in many people to be loyal to some form of royalty—a peasant complex. Or perhaps our cultural heritage has us well conditioned to grant the owners of a business (the family) great latitude in running it. "It's their business!"

There are still many family dynasties in big

business: Weyerhaeuser, Ford, Johnson (wax), to
name a few.

We have in Italy the example of the Duke of Ferrara,
who was able to withstand the assaults of the Venetians in
1484 and of Pope Julius in 1510, for no other reason than
because of the antiquity of his family in that dominion. In as
much as the legitimate prince has less cause and less necessity to give offence, it is only natural that he should be more
loved; and, if no extraordinary vices make him hated, it is
only reasonable for his subjects to be naturally attached to
him, the memories and causes of innovations being forgotten in the long period over which his rule has extended;
whereas one change always leaves the way prepared for the
introduction of another.

The Way to Govern Cities or Dominions That, Previous to Being Occupied, Lived Under Their Own Laws

WHEN THOSE states which have been acquired are accustomed to live at liberty under their own laws, there are three ways of holding them. *The first is to despoil them; the second is to go and live there in person; the third is to allow them to live under their own laws, taking tribute of them, and creating within the country a government composed of a few who will keep it friendly to you.*

A management that acquires companies also has these three choices:

7

1. Despoil the company (liquidate the assets, in more modern terminology). While admittedly rare these days, there are still instances in which an acquired property is worth more in liquidation than it is as an operating enterprise. An astute management will recognize such a situation and act accordingly, despite the cries of outrage that will be voiced by displaced employees. Lest their cries for mercy touch you, just remember that in many instances the company has a low value as an operating enterprise because these people have not been very good at their jobs. More commonly, "despoiling" the company will take the form of firing those people who seem to be incompetent or who are not needed and of selling off segments of the operation that are economic handicaps. While a thorough housecleaning sounds dreadful, consider the case of a company that suffered declining sales volume and profits for eight years and incurred substantial losses during the last two of these years. The company was sold to a firm that installed a new president. Within two months, he had:

   a. fired all of the vice presidents;
   b. fired the controller and hired a new one;
   c. hired a new sales manager;
   d. persuaded old members of the board of directors to give him free rein;
   e. reduced the number of employees from 650 to 550;
   f. brought in 17 new men at various management levels.

A rather good run at cleaning house! Results: gross margin up from 27% to 33%; profits in six months. The president, in explaining why he was able to use drastic techniques, said, "The company was sick and everyone knew it."

2. Go live there in person; move your management team in and run the operation.

3. Take tribute; leave the existing management alone as long as it forwards specified tribute (money) as budgeted. Experience indicates, however, that this delightful alternative is often short-lived for a number of reasons. Sometimes the acquiring company simply cannot keep hands off. Other times existing management fails to perform as expected.

Because this government, being created by the prince, knows that it cannot exist without his friendship and protection, [it] will do all it can to keep them. *What is more, a city used to liberty can be more easily held by means of its citizens than in any other way, if you wish to preserve it.*

If the employees of a company have enjoyed considerable "liberty" in the past—a management that has been permissive, democratic, or whatever you prefer to call it—and if you wish to preserve that organization, then you will have to cater to those people. Remove their traditional liberties and you are likely to be faced with building a new organization.

A new sales manager took over the reins of a paper wholesaler's sales force. He noted that his men behaved in ways to which he was unaccustomed. They worked the hours that pleased them, parked in convenient places in front of the warehouse, went fishing when the urge overcame them, and dressed very casually.

Orders were posted: All men were to report for work

at 8:00 A.M. dressed in conservative business suits. All cars were to be parked at the far end of the lot. There were many other changes along similar lines.

Over the next three months, the sales manager lost half of his men. This did not displease him, for he had little wish to preserve that organization. But he lost the *best* men and sales suffered. The owner fired the sales manager after six months. Reason: poor sales performance.

If you don't want to preserve one organization, have a better one on hand to take its place—or someone will be taking yours.

Of New Dominions Which Have Been Acquired by One's Own Arms and Ability

LET NO one marvel if in speaking of new dominions both as to prince and state; I bring forward very exalted instances, for men walk almost always in the paths trodden by others, proceeding in their actions by imitation. Not being always able to follow others exactly, nor attain to the excellence of those he imitates, *a prudent man should always follow in the path trodden by great men and imitate those who are most excellent, so that if he does not attain to their greatness, at any rate he will get some tinge of it.*

11

Sometimes it works, sometimes it doesn't. Once upon a time, a famous football coach was blessed with a talented All-American quarterback who worshiped the hallowed gridiron upon which the coach trod. After graduation, the quarterback returned to the scene of his collegiate glory as an assistant coach. Casual observers could scarcely discern the difference between coach and pupil: They walked alike and talked alike; they were as one. The assistant coach was a most apt pupil.

And it came to pass that the pupil became head coach at another, less athletically endowed institution of alleged learning. He proceeded to install a carbon copy of his idol's program. He mimicked his idol's coaching techniques, but they didn't work as well. Eventually he was forced to develop his own leadership style, but it was always affected.

The same famous coach was twice blessed. He had another All-American quarterback who became an assistant coach and subsequently a head coach. This pupil was a fantastic success. His creed: "A man's got to be himself. Copying someone else just won't work."

Ironically, the first pupil was never able to conquer his mentor, while the second knew nothing but victory.

But this type of exception glosses over what Machiavelli was really saying. The key words in his passage are *prudent man*, with an accent on the *prudent*. Niccolò was pointing out that it simply is not prudent (wise) to follow courses of action that have been avoided previously by men of proven wisdom and ability. True, you may be able to win by pioneering new paths, but such behavior is still not *prudent*: It is adventuresome. Bear in mind that a prudent man is a conservative animal. He seeks no avoidable risks. Prudent men plod proven paths.

He will do as prudent archers, who when the place they wish to hit is too far off, knowing how far their bow will carry, aim at a spot much higher than the one they wish to hit, not in order to reach this height with their arrow, but by help of this high aim to hit the spot they wish to.

I say then that in new dominions, where there is a new prince, it is more or less easy to hold them, according to the greater or lesser ability of him who acquires them. And as the fact of a private individual becoming a prince pre-supposes either great ability or good fortune, it would appear that either of these things would in part mitigate many difficulties. *Nevertheless those who have been less beholden to good fortune have maintained themselves best.*

While luck may play a critical role in rising to power, talent is usually needed to maintain it. But therein arises a problem: What portion of luck is but a disguise for talent? Unquestionably, people without talent seem to have more than their share of "bad luck." As football coaches are wont to shout, "You make your own luck!"

A young college graduate accepted employment as a salesman with a large oil field supply company. A sudden rash of automobile accidents subsequently resulted in the deaths of his bosses. He found himself regional sales manager, solely because he was the only man left in the area with any managerial preten-tions. But it was too soon. He wasn't ready for the job. Failure was fast in finding his doorstep. Several years later he had developed the requisite talents and made it back to top management.

The matter is also facilitated by the prince being obliged to reside personally in his territory, having no others. But to come to those who have become princes through their own merits and not by fortune, I regard as the greatest, Moses, Cyrus, Romulus, Theseus, and their like. And although one should not speak of Moses, he having merely carried out what was ordered him by God, still he deserves admiration, if only for that grace which made him worthy to speak with God. But regarding Cyrus and others who have acquired or founded kingdoms, they will all be found worthy of admiration; and if their particular actions and methods are examined they will not appear very different from those of Moses, although he had so great a Master. And in examining their life and deeds it will be seen that they owed nothing to fortune but the opportunity which gave them matter to be shaped into what form they thought fit; and without that opportunity their powers would have been wasted, and without their powers the opportunity would have come in vain.

It was thus necessary that Moses should find the people of Israel slaves in Egypt and oppressed by the Egyptians, so that they were disposed to follow him in order to escape from their servitude. It was necessary that Romulus should be unable to remain in Alba, and should have been exposed at his birth, in order that he might become King of Rome and founder of that nation. It was necessary that Cyrus should find the Persians discontented with the empire of the Medes, and the Medes weak and effeminate through long peace. Theseus could not have shown his abilities if he had not found the Athenians dispersed. These opportunities, therefore, gave these men their chance, and their own great qualities enabled them to profit by them, so as to ennoble their country and augment its fortunes.

Those who by the exercise of abilities such as these become princes, obtain their dominions with difficulty but retain them easily, and the difficulties which they have in acquiring their dominions arise in part from the new rules and regulations that they have to introduce in order to establish their position securely. *It must be considered that there is nothing more difficult to carry out, nor more doubtful of success, nor more dangerous to handle, than to initiate a new order of things.*

And here we have a most important administrative insight. The managerial graveyard is strewn with the career corpses of eager new administrators who have accepted their positions full of hope and ideas for organizational improvements. People know what they have with the status quo and are fearful of losing it—no matter how meager it may be—under a proposed new order. Few employees have sufficient vision to confidently foretell how they will fare under new circumstances. Moreover, some will accurately perceive that their positions in the organization will be damaged under the new order. Only those who clearly see that it is to their advantage will support the change.

Or let's consider it from another aspect—that of acceptance or conditioning. Employees of a going enterprise have come to accept certain procedures as the "right" way. They have been conditioned. Those who do not accept the existing managerial styles are usually weeded out rather rapidly.

In comes the new manager with new ways—ways that go against the existing pattern of acceptance. If you will, the people have been programmed for one managerial style; they find it difficult to reprogram themselves for the new order of things without considerable resistance.

Predictably, employees who have been with the organization the shortest length of time can accommodate the new leader better than the old timers.

A new dean with progressive ideas assumed control of a large, significant school. He tried to introduce several new programs, but was met with overt resistance from the older faculty and from associate deans who were in senior positions. He was forced to turn to the young, newly hired faculty for support, several of whom had advanced rapidly into positions of administrative responsiblility. To no avail, however; he was forced out by a conspiracy of the older men.

For the reformer has enemies in all those who profit by the old order, and only lukewarm defenders in all those who would profit by the new order, this lukewarmness arising partly from fear of their adversaries, who have the laws in their favour; and partly from the incredulity of mankind, who do not truly believe in anything new until they have had actual experience of it. Thus it arises that on every opportunity for attacking the reformer, his opponents do so with the zeal of partisans [and] the others only defend him half-heartedly, so that between them he runs great danger. It is necessary, however, in order to investigate thoroughly this question, to examine whether these innovators are independent, or whether they depend upon others; that is to say, whether in order to carry out their designs they have to entreat or are able to compel. In the first case they invariably succeed ill, and accomplish nothing; but when they can depend on their own strength and are able to use force, they rarely fail. *Thus it comes about that all armed prophets have conquered and unarmed ones failed . . .*

Make sure you have the guns before you go to war. Diplomacy sometimes is a fancy word for idle or empty talk. The new administrator should make certain of his power base before instituting his plans, for he will be forced to weather some organizational storms that will swamp him if he has been lax in securing his position.

An investor bought a minority position in a small chain of women's apparel stores and was given some managerial responsibilities. He had some great plans for the enterprise, but was frustrated by resistance from the other investors. As he had no real power base, they were able to squeeze him out. He threatened their position. He later bought control of a sick store, where he instituted his programs successfully. He had the power to compel obedience: Opponents were fired.

. . . for besides what has been already said, the character of peoples varies, and it is easy to persuade them of a thing, but difficult to keep them in that persuasion. And so it is necessary to order things so that when they no longer believe, they can be made to believe by force. Moses, Cyrus, Theseus, and Romulus would not have been able to keep their constitutions observed for so long had they been disarmed, as happened in our own time with Fra Girolamo Savonarola, who failed entirely in his new rule when the multitude began to disbelieve in him, and he had no means of holding fast those who had believed nor of compelling

the unbelievers to believe. Therefore such men as these
have great difficulty in making their way, and all their
dangers are met on the road and must be overcome by their
own abilities; but when once they have overcome them and
have begun to be held in veneration, and have suppressed
those who envied them, they remain powerful and secure,
honoured and happy.

To the high examples given I will add a lesser one,
which, however, is in some measure comparable and will
serve as an instance of all such cases, that of Hiero of
Syracuse, who from a private individual became Prince of
Syracuse, without other aid from fortune beyond the opportunity; for the Syracusans being oppressed, elected him
as their captain, from which post he rose by ability to be
prince; while still in private life his virtues were such that it
was written of him, that he lacked nothing to reign but the
kingdom. He abolished the old militia, raised a new one,
abandoned his old friendships and formed others; and as he
had thus friends and soldiers of his own choosing, he was
able on this foundation to build securely, so that while he
had great trouble in acquiring his position he had little in
maintaining it.

Of New Dominions
Acquired by
the Power of Others
or by Fortune

THOSE WHO *rise from private citizens to be princes merely by fortune have little trouble in rising but very much in maintaining their position.*

With a great deal of good fortune, one famous man rose to the presidency of a large consumer goods organization. When fortune deserted him, forcing him to rely on ability and judgment, he was fired. His astounding series of blunders almost ruined the company, and it subsequently never really regained its

position in the industry. The man's business acumen
was so poor that he could not get a top management
position elsewhere, so he went into an entirely different profession—the one for which he was originally
trained.

Those who rely on luck will come to ruin, as Dame
Fortune is fickle and eventually bestows her affections
upon others—usually those with talent.

They meet with no difficulties on the way as they fly over
them, but all their difficulties arise when they are established. Such are they who are granted a state either for
money, or by favour of him who grants it, as happened to
many in Greece, in the cities of Ionia and of the Helles-
pont, who were created princes by Darius in order to hold
these places for his security and glory; such were also those
emperors who from private citizens rose to power by brib-
ing the army. *Such as these depend absolutely on the good
will and fortune of those who have raised them, both of
which are extremely inconstant and unstable.*

Perhaps the position of the managers and coaches of
professional sports teams is the best illustration of this
point: They are at the mercy of their sponsors.

They neither know how to, nor are in a position to
maintain their rank, for unless he be a man of great genius
it is not likely that one who has always lived in a private
position should know how to command, and they are unable to maintain themselves because they possess no

forces friendly and faithful to them. Moreover, states quickly founded, like all other things of rapid beginnings and growth, cannot have deep roots and wide ramifications, so that the first storm destroys them, unless, as already said, the man who thus becomes a prince is of such great genius as to be able to take immediate steps for maintaining what fortune has thrown into his lap, and lay afterwards those foundations which others make before becoming princes.

With regard to these two methods of becoming a prince, by ability or by good fortune, I will here adduce two examples which have occurred within our memory, those of Francesco Sforza and Cesare Borgia. Francesco, by appropriate means and through great abilities, from citizen became Duke of Milan, and what he had attained after a thousand difficulties he maintained with little trouble. On the other hand, Cesare Borgia, commonly called Duke Valentine, acquired the state by the influence of his father and lost it when that influence failed, and that although every measure was adopted by him and everything done that a prudent and capable man could do to establish himself firmly in a state that the arms and the favours of others had given him. For, as we have said, he who does not lay his foundations beforehand may by great abilities do so afterwards, although with great trouble to the architect and danger to the building. If, then, one considers the procedure of the duke, it will be seen how firm were the foundations he had laid to his future power, which I do not think is superfluous to examine, as I know of no better precepts for a new prince to follow than may be found in his actions; and if his measures were not successful, it was through no fault of his own but only by the most extraordinary malignity of fortune.

Of Those Who Have Attained the Position of Prince by Villainy

BUT AS there are still two ways of becoming prince which cannot be attributed entirely either to fortune or to ability, they must not be passed over, although one of them could be more fully discussed if we were treating of republics. These are when one becomes prince by some nefarious or villainous means, or when a private citizen becomes the prince of his country through the favour of his fellow-citizens. And in speaking of the former means, I will give two examples, one ancient, the other modern, without entering further into the merits of this method, as I judge them to be sufficient for any one obliged to imitate them.

Agathocles the Sicilian rose not only from private life but from the lowest and most abject position to be King of Syracuse. The son of a potter, he led a life of the utmost wickedness through all the stages of his fortune. Nevertheless, his wickedness was accompanied by such vigour of mind and body that, having joined the militia, he rose through its ranks to be praetor of Syracuse. Having been appointed to this position, and having decided to become prince and to hold with violence and without the support of others that which had been constitutionally granted him; and having imparted his design to Hamilcar the Carthaginian, who was fighting with his armies in Sicily, he called together one morning the people and senate of Syracuse, as if he had to deliberate on matters of importance to the republic, and at a given signal had all the senators and the richest men of the people killed by his soldiers. After their death he occupied and held rule over the city without any civil strife. And although he was twice beaten by the Carthaginians and ultimately besieged, he was able not only to defend the city, but leaving a portion of his forces for its defence, with the remainder he invaded Africa, and in a short time liberated Syracuse from the siege and brought the Carthaginians to great extremities, so that they were obliged to come to terms with him, and remain contented with the possession of Africa, leaving Sicily to Agathocles. Whoever considers, therefore, the actions and qualities of this man, will see few if any things which can be attributed to fortune; for, as above stated, it was not by the favour of any person, but through the grades of the militia, in which he had advanced with a thousand hardships and perils, that he arrived at the position of prince, which he afterwards maintained by so many courageous and perilous expedients. *It cannot be called virtue to kill one's fellow-*

citizens, betray one's friends, be without faith, without pity, and without religion: by these methods one may indeed gain power, but not glory.

Clearly, Machiavelli held no brief for such contemptible behavior, but in the name of accurate reporting he was compelled to present and evaluate it. Niccolò's critics would have you believe that he glorified the exploits of such despots.

For if the virtues of Agathocles in braving and overcoming perils, and his greatness of soul in supporting and surmounting obstacles be considered, one sees no reason for holding him inferior to any of the most renowned captains. Nevertheless his barbarous cruelty and inhumanity, together with his countless atrocities, do not permit of his being named among the most famous men. We cannot attribute to fortune or virtue that which he achieved without either.

In our own times, during the pontificate of Alexander VI, Oliverotto da Fermo had been left as a young fatherless boy under the care of his maternal uncle, Giovanni Fogliani, who brought him up, and sent him in early youth to soldier under Paolo Vitelli, in order that he might, trained in that hard school, obtain a good military position. On the death of Paolo he fought under his brother Vitellozzo, and in a very short time, being of great intelligence, and active in mind and body, he became one of the leaders of his troops. But deeming it servile to be under others, he resolved, with the help of some citizens of Fermo, who preferred servitude to the liberty of their country, and with

the favour of the Vitelli, to occupy Fermo; he therefore
wrote to Giovanni Fogliani, how, having been for many
years away from home, he wished to come to see him
and his city, and as far as possible to inspect his estates.
And as he had only laboured to gain honour, in order
that his fellow-citizens might see that he had not spent
his time in vain, he wished to come honourably accompanied by one hundred horsemen, his friends and followers, and prayed him that he would be pleased to order
that he should be received with honour by the citizens
of Fermo, by which he would honour not only him,
Oliverotto, but also himself, as he had been his pupil.
Giovanni did not fail in any due courtesy towards his
nephew; he caused him to be honourably received by the
people of Fermo, and lodged him in his own house. After
waiting some days to arrange all that was necessary to his
villainous projects, Oliverotto invited Giovanni Fogliani
and all the principal men of Fermo to a grand banquet.
After the dinner and the entertainments usual at such
feasts, Oliverotto artfully introduced certain important
matters of discussion, speaking of the greatness of Pope
Alexander, and of his son Cesare, and of their enterprises.
To which discourses Giovanni and others having replied,
he all at once rose, saying that these matters should be
spoken of in a more private place, and withdrew into a
room where Giovanni and the other citizens followed him.
They were no sooner seated than soldiers rushed out of
hiding places and killed Giovanni and all the others. After
which massacre Oliverotto mounted his horse, rode
through the town and besieged the chief magistrate in
his place, so that through fear they were obliged to obey
him and form a government, of which he made

himself prince. And all those being dead who, if discontented, could injure him, he fortified himself with new orders, civil and military, in such a way that within the year that he held the principality he was not only safe himself in the city of Fermo but had become formidable to all his neighbours. And his overthrow would have been difficult, like that of Agathocles, if he had not allowed himself to be deceived by Cesare Borgia, when he captured the Orsini and Vitelli at Sinigaglia, as already related, where he also was taken, one year after the parricide he had committed, and strangled, together with Vitellozzo, who had been his teacher in ability and atrocity.

Some may wonder how it came about that Agathocles, and others like him, could, after infinite treachery and cruelty, live secure for many years in their country and defend themselves from external enemies without being conspired against by their subjects; although many others have, owing to their cruelty, been unable to maintain their position in times of peace, not to speak of the uncertain times of war. I believe this arises from the cruelties being exploited well or badly. *Well committed may be called those (if it is permissible to use the word well of evil) which are perpetrated once for the need of securing one's self, and which afterwards are not persisted in but are exchanged for measures as useful to the subjects as possible. Cruelties ill committed are those which, although at first few, increase rather than diminish with time.* Those who follow the former method may remedy in some measure their condition, both with God and man; as did Agathocles. As to the others, it is impossible for them to maintain themselves.

Whence it is to be noted, that in taking a state the *conqueror must arrange to commit all his cruelties at once,*

so as not to recur to them every day, and so as to be able, by
not making fresh changes, to reassure people and win them
over by benefiting them.

Good advice for the new administrator! One able executive who had been made responsible for improving the performance of a large company studied the operation for awhile before making his move. Once he saw what had to be done, he acted: He fired 23 incompetents, made some organizational rearrangements, and told the survivors that they had made his team. The blood bath was over. Secure in their positions, the survivors closed ranks behind him.

An investor-manager bought a small company that manufactured a line of outdoor sporting equipment. While the firm was profitable, the investor was informed of several serious personnel problems by both the former owner and a consultant the new owner had retained to evaluate the enterprise before buying it. Upon assuming command he announced, "For the time being, there will be no personnel changes. I want to study the operation for awhile."

As each "problem" became clear to him, he fired it. The employees were very insecure, to say the least. Each Friday saw someone released. Then one Friday the foreman of the plant resigned, saying: "I've been made an offer by ———— [a competitor]. I'm going to take it."

The foreman was the best man in the plant, and the owner did not want to lose him. He tried to talk the foreman out of it, but it was too late. He had been alienated by the owner's managerial tactics.

No organization can function properly under a continual reign of terror. Employees must be able to concentrate on the work that must be done, and not have their minds possessed by fears for their own security.

Whoever acts otherwise, either through timidity or bad counsel, is always obliged to stand with knife in hand, and can never depend on his subjects, because they, owing to continually fresh injuries, are unable to depend upon him. *For injuries should be done all together, so that being less tasted, they will give less offence. Benefits should be granted little by little, so that they may be better enjoyed.*

"But what have you done for me lately?" That punch line from the old joke nicely summarizes the problems inherent in bestowing benefits upon people. Memories not only are short, but they set precedents.

The owner of a service station hired a promising young man to manage it. Things went well. Three months later, the owner said, "Joe, you're doing a great job. I want to give you a raise and some fringe benefits. I am going to give you everything I can right now, so you can enjoy it now rather than string it out over a period of time."

Joe was delighted. But six months later, Joe said, "Boss, I haven't had a raise for some time now. Cost of living is up, you know."

Now, try to tell Joe that he was given that raise six months ago. No way!

Many small rewards seem to provide more incentive than the same total reward in one bundle. Try it on your spouse!

And above all, a prince must live with his subjects in such a way that no accident of good or evil fortune can deflect him from his course; for necessity arising in adverse times, you are not in time with severity, and the good that you do does not profit, as it is judged to be forced upon you, and you will derive no benefit whatever from it.

Of the
Civic Principality

BUT WE now come to the case where a citizen becomes prince not through crime or intolerable violence, but by the favour of his fellow-citizens, which may be called a civic principality. To attain this position depends not entirely on worth or entirely on fortune, but rather on cunning assisted by fortune. One attains it by help of popular favour or by the favour of the aristocracy. For in every city these two opposite parties are to be found, arising from the desire of the populace to avoid the oppression of the great, and the desire of the great to command and oppress the people. And from these two opposing interests arises in

the city one of the three effects: either absolute
government, liberty, or licence. The former is created
either by the populace or the nobility, depending on the
relative opportunities of the two parties; for when the
nobility see that they are unable to resist the people, they
unite in exalting one of their number and creating him
prince, so as to be able to carry out their own designs under
the shadow of his authority. The populace, on the other
hand, when unable to resist the nobility, endeavour to
exalt and create a prince in order to be protected by his
authority. *He who becomes prince by help of the nobility
has greater difficulty in maintaining his power than he who
is raised by the populace, for he is surrounded by those who
think themselves his equals, and is thus unable to direct or
command as he pleases. But one who is raised to leadership
by popular favour finds himself alone, and has no one, or
very few, who are not ready to obey him.*

The deanship of a school of business was open. The
top administration was about to promote the school's
most noted professor—a man of strong administrative
bent—when a coalition of the school's full professors
(nobility, if you will) went to the president with a petition
to give the deanship to another man—a rather meek
person of moderate talent. The president acquiesced.
For years thereafter the organization went nowhere.
The dean was owned by his full professors, and they
opted for the status quo.

This passage raises some interesting questions
about "people's democracies." Machiavelli suggests
that those rulers who are installed by the people
thereafter do not have to do much for them. Perhaps
this explains some of the behavior of communistically
inclined governments.

Besides which, it is impossible to satisfy the nobility by fair dealing and without inflicting injury on others, whereas it is very easy to satisfy the mass of the people in this way. *For the aim of the people is more honest than that of the nobility, the latter desiring to oppress, and the former merely to avoid oppression.*

Now, does that sound like a villain talking?

It must also be added that the prince can never insure himself against a hostile populace on account of their number, but he can against the hostility of the great, as they are but few. The worst that a prince has to expect from a hostile people is to be abandoned, but from hostile nobles he has to fear not only desertion but their active opposition, and as they are more far-seeing and more cunning, they are always in time to save themselves and take sides with the one who they expect will conquer. *The prince is, moreover, obliged to live always with the same people, but he can easily do without the same nobility, being able to make and unmake them at any time, and improve their position or deprive them of it as he pleases.*

Assistants, take note! If you present your boss with a dilemma which forces him to sacrifice either you or his "people," it would be prudent for you to have in mind where you will work next. It is far easier to replace one man than many.

And to throw further light on this part of my argument, I would say, that the nobles are to be considered in two different manners; that is, they are either to be ruled so as to make them entirely dependent on your fortunes, or else not. Those that are thus bound to you and are not rapacious, must be honoured and loved; those who stand aloof must be considered in two ways, they either do this through pusillanimity and natural want of courage, and in this case you ought to make use of them, and especially such as are of good counsel, so that they may honour you in prosperity and in adversity you have not to fear them. But when they are not bound to you of set purpose and for ambitious ends, it is a sign that they think more of themselves than of you; and from such men the prince must guard himself and look upon them as secret enemies, who will help to ruin him when in adversity.

One, however, who becomes prince by favour of the populace, must maintain its friendship, which he will find easy, the people asking nothing but not to be oppressed. But one who against the people's wishes becomes prince by favour of the nobles, *should above all endeavour to gain the favour of the people; this will be easy to him if he protects them.*

Most important: subordinates want protection from attack by others in the organization. They will accept deserved criticism from their immediate supervisor, but expect in return to be free from harassment from other executives in the organization. And they expect their boss to go to bat for them when the occasion warrants. Woe to the manager who fails to support (fight for) his group when the need arises.

The faculty of a certain school approved the

appointment of a dean who was strongly supported by
the university's president, in the belief that he would be
able to compete successfully for institutional resources because of his relationship with the top administrator. The faculty members were disappointed.
The new dean did nothing for them. His allegiance was
not to the faculty but to the administrator, upon whom
he placed few demands.

And as men, who receive good from whom they
expected evil, feel under a greater obligation to their
benefactor, so the populace will soon become even better
disposed towards him than if he had become prince
through their favour. The prince can win their favour in
many ways, which vary according to circumstances, for
which no certain rule can be given, and will therefore be
passed over. I will only say, in conclusion, that it is
*necessary for a prince to possess the friendship of the
people; otherwise he has no resource in times of adversity.*

To continue with the story of the dean, all went well
with him until his sponsor, the president, resigned.
Matters then became increasingly difficult for him, and
the new president finally asked him to resign. Few
protests were heard from the faculty, some of whom
had actually helped to precipitate his resignation.

Nabis, prince of the Spartans, sustained a siege by the
whole of Greece and a victorious Roman army, and defended his country against them and maintained his own
position. It sufficed when the danger arose for him to make

sure of a few, which would not have sufficed if the populace had been hostile to him. *And let no one oppose my opinion in this by quoting the trite proverb, "He who builds on the people, builds on mud"; because that is true when a private citizen relies upon the people and persuades himself that they will liberate him if he is oppressed by enemies or by the magistrates . . .*

An administrator can build on the people; a fellow worker cannot. One aggressively able but abrasive young man deliberately continued a running feud with his foreman, who could be described at best as marginal. The young man's fellow workers held his hand and dried his tears after each fight, but none of them came to his aid when the foreman managed to fire him with no recommendation. Don't expect help from your fellow workers in a fight with management. It's every man for himself.

. . . in this case he might often find himself deceived, as were in Rome the Gracchi and in Florence Messer Georgio Scali. But when it is a prince who founds himself on this basis, one who can command, and is a man of courage, and does not get frightened in adversity, and does not neglect other preparations, and one who by his own valour and measures animates the mass of the people, he will not find himself deceived by them, and he will find that he has laid his foundations well.

Usually these principalities are in danger when the prince changes from the position of civil ruler to an absolute one, for these princes either command themselves or by means of magistrates. In the latter case, their position is weaker and more dangerous, for they are at the mercy of those citizens who are appointed magistrates, who can, especially in times of adversity, with great facility deprive them of their position, either by acting against them or by not obeying them. The prince is not quick enough in such dangers, to assume absolute authority, for the citizens and subjects who are accustomed to take their orders from the magistrates are not ready in these emergencies to obey his, and he will always in difficult times lack men whom he can rely on. Such a prince cannot base himself on what he sees in quiet times, when the citizens have need of the state; for then every one is full of promises and each one is ready to die for him when death is far off; but in adversity, when the state has need of citizens, then he will find but few. And this experience is the more dangerous, in that it can only be had once. *Therefore a wise prince will seek means by which his subjects will always and in every possible condition of things have need of his government, and then they will always be faithful to him.*

If your people come to the conclusion that they don't need you, watch out! The golf pro at a rather well-to-do private club was indifferent to the needs of the members. He offered no leadership in the club's golf program and showed scant interest in improving members' golfing skills. Eventually someone asked the board, "So, who needs him?" No answer was found, so a new pro was.

How the Strength of All States Should Be Measured

IN EXAMINING the character of these principalities it is necessary to consider another point, namely, whether the prince has such position as to be able in case of need to maintain himself alone, or whether he has always need of the protection of others. The better to explain this I would say, that I consider those capable of maintaining themselves alone who can, through abundance of men or money, put together a sufficient army, and hold the field against any one who assails them; and I consider to have need of others, those who cannot take the field against their enemies, but are obliged to take refuge within their walls and stand on the defensive. . . . In the second case, there is nothing to be said except to encourage such a prince to provision and fortify his own town, and not to trouble about the surrounding country. And whoever has strongly fortified his town and, as regards the government of his subjects, has proceeded as we have already described and will further relate, will be attacked with great reluctance, *for men are always averse to enterprises in which they foresee difficulties, and it can never appear easy to attack one who has his town stoutly defended and is not hated by the people.*

A new products development manager was faced with deciding which of two products should be introduced to the market. The one which would have to invade a market in which three tough competitors were well entrenched was dropped in favor of the item that would be up against weak competition.

Corporate adventurers look not to strong enterprises for their forays, but seek enterprises that can be easily taken. The administrator who wants to avoid proxy fights or takeovers should continually maintain his defenses against such attacks.

The tale of the late Seward Avery, former president of Montgomery Ward, is legendary. Avery worked long and hard to put his company in a highly liquid cash position to gain the advantage in a depression he was certain would come. Result: His empire was attacked and taken over by entrepreneurs attracted to his cash. People are attracted to cash as bears are to honey. His employees were of no help to him for he was "hated."

But there are other tales of corporate woe that are not so well publicized. An able young entrepreneur took over a faltering metal parts manufacturing concern whose stock was traded publicly. He cut costs, marshaled cash and assets, and made money—lots of it. But he paid no heed to his stockholders: there were no dividends, no public relations to boost the price of the stock. The price of the stock slid well below hard book value. Some sharpies began buying the stock slyly. In three years, they owned the company for a fraction of its worth. Then the president was given a new set of rules to play by; the new game was called "let's run up the price of our stock." Not wanting to play this new game, he looked for a new employer—his work of five years down the drain. He had failed to make his empire safe from attack.

The care and feeding of stockholders is as much a part of the job of the president of a corporation as sales and production. In this era of "stockholders be damned," such advice is easily cast aside. And the chances are good that you can get away with it, but if you're wrong you can lose your empire.

The best defense from stockholder attacks is a stock price high in relation to the true value behind it. As cynical as it may be, price is frequently not a result of the economic circumstances of the enterprise, but rather of management's adeptness at selling the stock-buying public the idea that the firm has a glowing future. A pound of future seems to be worth about three pounds of present.

The cities of Germany are absolutely free, have little surrounding country, and obey the emperor when they choose, and they do no fear him or any other potentate that they have about them. They are fortified in such a manner that every one thinks that to reduce them would be tedious and difficult, for they all have the necessary moats and bastions, sufficient artillery, and always keep food, drink, and fuel for one year in the public storehouses. Beyond which, to keep the lower classes satisfied and without loss to the commonwealth, they have always enough means to give them work for one year in these employments which form the nerve and life of the town, and in the industries by which the lower classes live. Military exercises are still held in high reputation, and many regulations are in force for maintaining them.

A prince, therefore, who possesses a strong city and does not make himself hated, cannot be assaulted; and if he were to be so, the assailant would be obliged to retire shamefully; for so many things change, that it is almost impossible for any one to maintain a siege for a year with his armies idle. And to those who urge that the people, having their possessions outside and seeing them burnt, will not have patience, and the long siege and self-interest will make them forget their prince, I reply that a powerful and courageous prince will always overcome those difficulties by now raising the hopes of his subjects that the evils will not last long, now impressing them with fear of the enemy's cruelty, now by dextrously assuring himself of those who appear too bold. Besides which, the enemy would naturally burn and ravage the country on first arriving and at the time when men's minds are still hot and eager to defend themselves, and therefore the prince has still less to fear, for after some time, when people have cooled down, the damage is done, the evil has been suffered, and there is no remedy, so that they are the more ready to unite with their prince, as it appears that he is under an obligation to them, their houses having been burnt and their possessions ruined in his defence.

It is the nature of men to be as much bound by the

benefits that they confer as by those they receive. From which it follows that, everything considered, a prudent prince will not find it difficult to uphold the courage of his subjects both at the commencement and during a state of siege, if he possesses provisions and means to defend himself.

The Different Kinds of Militia and Mercenary Soldiers

HAVING NOW discussed fully the qualities of these principalities of which I proposed to treat, and partially considered the causes of their prosperity or failure, and having also showed the methods by which many have sought to obtain such states, it now remains for me to treat generally of the methods, both offensive and defensive, that can be used in each of them. We have said already how necessary it is for a prince to have his foundations good, otherwise he is certain to be ruined. The chief foundations of all states, whether new, old, or mixed, are good laws and good arms. And as there cannot be good laws where there are not good arms, and where there are good arms there must be good laws, I will not now discuss the laws, but will speak of the arms.

I say, therefore, that the arms by which a prince defends his possessions are either his own, or else mercenaries, or auxiliaries, or mixed. *The mercenaries and auxiliaries are useless and dangerous, and if any one supports his state by the arms of mercenaries, he will never stand firm or sure, as they are disunited, ambitious, without discipline, faithless, bold amongst friends, cowardly amongst enemies, they have no fear of God, and keep no faith with men.*

The office equipment industry provides a case in point. Historically, the first typewriter manufacturers (Underwood, Royal, Smith-Corona) used independent distributors and dealers—mercenaries. Then came IBM and its company-owned distribution system. IBM's marketing organization was fearsome; it dominated the industry and established a distribution system that has subsequently been copied by others.

The problem with independent middlemen (mercenaries) is that one cannot rely on their performance. Some will be good; most will be mediocre.

Today's management strives for tight control over the performance of its "armies." It does not want to use mercenaries unless forced to do so by the economics of the situation. A company salesman who has gone sour can be replaced much more easily than a faulty distributor. A branch manager can be fired if the branch's performance is unsatisfactory, but it is not easy to replace a lax independent distributor.

However, the critic asks, "Isn't everyone in business a mercenary?" To varying degrees, yes! We work for money, and for that we are all mercenaries. But for some people—hopefully for many people—there are allegiances that transcend money. People do form attachments to other people, to companies, to communities, to ideas, and to causes. Some cynics pooh-pooh as sophomoric the apparent loyalty and enthusiasm some managers are able to generate in their subordinates. Yet, on every hand, we can see examples of such loyalties. Moreover, it is rather apparent that these non-monetary motives usually prove to be more powerful than monetary motives. The work of such notable management theorists as Herzberg, MacGregor, and Maslow has uniformly indicated the importance of non-monetary motives in worker performance.

Many managers shy away from the man whose sole loyalty is to his paycheck, for he can easily be lured away by another firm offering a larger check. The buck chaser seldom stays in one place for long and he seldom enjoys the personal relationships which are an important part of most successful organizations. While a manager can't expect his people to lay down their lives for him—a paycheck only buys so much—still he can try to avoid blatant mercenaries. Administrators are always seeking people who show some evidence of devotion to something other than the buck. Executives who expect more most likely will be disappointed. The problem is compounded by managers who are fanatically dedicated to their jobs and cannot understand people who do not share their motivation.

Ruin is only deferred as long as the assault is postponed; in peace you are despoiled by them [mercenaries], and in war by the enemy. *The cause of this is that they have no love or other motive to keep them in the field beyond a trifling wage, which is not enough to make them ready to die for you.* They are quite willing to be your soldiers so long as you do not make war, but when war comes, it is either fly or decamp altogether. I ought to have little trouble in proving this, since the ruin of Italy is now caused by nothing else but through her having relied for many years on mercenary arms. These did indeed help certain individuals to power, and appeared courageous when matched against each other, but when the foreigner came they showed their worthlessness. Thus it came about that King Charles of France was allowed to take Italy without the slightest trouble, and those who said that it was owing to our sins, spoke the truth, but it was not the sins they meant but those that I have related. And as it was the sins of princes, they too have suffered the punishment.

I will explain more fully the defects of these arms. *Mercenary captains are either very capable men or not; if they are, you cannot rely upon them, for they will always aspire to their own greatness, either by oppressing you, their master, or by oppressing others against your intentions; but if the captain is not an able man, he will generally ruin you.*

Perhaps the clearest instances illustrating this point involve those manufacturers who choose to use sales agents to market their wares. (A sales agent has the exclusive right to sell all of the manufacturer's output. He is the maker's sole means of selling his product.)

Now some sales agents are capable and some are not. An able agent is a joy to behold. He can take a product and move it into the market with most satisfying results. He knows the market; he knows his customers. But that is the point—they are *his* customers and *his* market. Thus the manufacturer who employs

such a talented agent quickly becomes enslaved by
him, dependent upon the continued flow of revenue to
which only the agent has the key.

On the other hand, should the manufacturer retain
an inept agent, the results will be insufficient to support
operations, and the manufacturer will be ruined.

Small wonder that many firms prefer to develop their
own "armies" to market their wares.

And if it is replied to this, that whoever has armed forces
will do the same, whether these are mercenary or not, I
would reply that as armies are to be used either by a prince
or by a republic, the prince must go in person to take the
position of captain, and the republic must send its own
citizens. If the man sent turns out incompetent, it must
change him; and if capable, keep him by law from going
beyond the proper limits. And it is seen by experience that
only princes and armed republics make very great progress, whereas mercenary forces do nothing but harm, and
also an armed republic submits less easily to the rule of one
of its citizens than a republic armed by foreign forces.

Rome and Sparta were for many centuries well armed
and free. The Swiss are well armed and enjoy great free-
dom. As an example of mercenary armies in antiquity there
are the Carthaginians, who were oppressed by their
mercenary soldiers, after the termination of the first war
with the Romans, even while they still had their own
citizens as captains. Philip of Macedon was made captain of
their forces by the Thebans after the death of Epaminondas, and after gaining the victory he deprived them of
liberty. The Milanese, on the death of Duke Philip, hired
Francesco Sforza against the Venetians, who having overcome the enemy at Caravaggio, allied himself with them to
oppress the Milanese, his own employers. The father of

this Sforza, being a soldier in the service of Queen Giovanna of Naples, left her suddenly unarmed, by which she was compelled, in order not to lose the kingdom, to throw herself into the arms of the King of Aragon. And if the Venetians and Florentines have in times past increased their dominions by means of such forces, and their captains have not made themselves princes but have defended them, I reply that the Florentines in this case have been favoured by chance, for of the capable leaders whom they might have feared, some did not conquer, some met with opposition, and others directed their ambition elsewhere. The one who did not conquer was Sir John Hawkwood, whose fidelity could not be known as he was not victorious, but every one will admit that, had he conquered, the Florentines would have been at his mercy. Sforza had always the Bracceschi against him which served as a mutual check. Francesco directed his ambition towards Lombardy; Braccio against the Church and the kingdom of Naples.

But let us look at what occurred a short time ago. The Florentines appointed Paolo Vitelli their captain, a man of great prudence, who had risen from a private station to the highest reputation. If he had taken Pisa, no one can deny that it was highly important for the Florentines to retain his friendship, because had he become the soldier of their enemies they would have had no means of opposing him; and if they had retained him they would have been obliged to obey him. As to the Venetians, if one considers the progress they made, it will be seen that they acted surely and gloriously so long as they made war with their own forces; that it was before they commenced their enterprises on land that they fought courageously with their own gentlemen and armed populace, but when they began to fight on land they abandoned this virtue, and began to follow the Italian custom. And at the commencement of their land conquests they had not much to fear from their captains, their territories not being very large, and their reputation being great, but as their possessions increased, as they did under Carmagnola, they had an example of their mistake. For seeing that he was very powerful, after he had defeated the Duke of Milan, and knowing, on the other hand, that he was but lukewarm in this war, they considered that they would not make any more conquests with him, and they neither would nor could dismiss him, for fear of losing what they had already gained. In order to make sure of him they were therefore obliged to execute him. They then had for captains Bartolommeo da Bergamo, Roberto da San Severino, Count di Pitigliano, and such like, from whom they had to fear loss instead of gain, as happened subsequently at Vailà, where in one day they lost what they had laboriously gained in eight hundred years; for with these forces, only slow and trifling acquisitions are made, but sudden and miraculous losses. And as I have cited these examples from Italy, which has now for many years been governed by mercenary forces, I will now deal more largely with them, so that having seen their origin and progress, they can be better remedied.

You must understand that in these latter times, as soon as the empire began to be repudiated in Italy and the Pope to gain greater reputation in temporal matters, Italy was divided into many states; many of the principal cities took up arms against their nobles, who, favoured by the emperor, had held them in subjection, and the Church encouraged this in order to increase its temporal power. In many other cities one of the inhabitants became prince. Thus Italy having fallen almost entirely into the hands of the Church and a few republics, and the priests and other citizens not being accustomed to bear arms, they began to hire foreigners as soldiers. The first to bring into reputation this kind of militia was Alberigo da Como, a native of Romagna. Braccio and Sforza, who were in their day the arbiters of Italy were, amongst others, trained by him. After these came all those others who up to the present day have commanded the armies of Italy, and the result of their prowess has been that Italy has been overrun by Charles, preyed on by Louis, tyrannised by Ferrando, and insulted by the Swiss. The system adopted by them was, in the first place, to increase their own reputation by discrediting the infantry. They did this because, as they had no country and lived on their earnings, a few foot soldiers did not augment their reputation, and they could not maintain a large number and therefore they restricted themselves almost entirely to cavalry, by which with a smaller number they were well paid and honoured. They reduced things to such a state that in an army of 20,000 soldiers there were not 2,000 foot. They had also used every means to spare themselves and the soldiers any hardship or fear by not killing each other in their encounters, but taking prisoners without expectation of ransom. They made no attacks on fortifications by night; and those in the fortifications did not attack the tents at night, they made no stockades or ditches around their camps, and did not take the field in winter. All these things were permitted by their military code, and adopted, as we have said, to avoid trouble and danger, so that they have reduced Italy to slavery and degradation.

The strategic aspects underlying Italy's downfall should not be overlooked by top management. The Italians divided their enterprise into many small units,

none of which could defend itself because of the terrible state into which its army had degenerated.

Not so many years ago, the decentralization of operations was a managment fad. Many small units of several large corporations, some conglomerates, were to operate as independent enterprises. Obviously, there are a great many advantages to such decentralization, but the strategy does seem to include the risk that a smaller, independent unit may prove unable to take care of itself before central management can remedy the matter.

The history of the United States is a good example of the strength gained by union.

The Duties of a Prince with Regard to the Militia

A PRINCE should therefore have no other aim or thought, nor take up any other thing for his study, but war and its organisation and discipline, for that is the only art that is necessary to one who commands, and it is of such virtue that it not only maintains those who are born princes, but often enables men of private fortune to attain to that rank. And one sees, on the other hand, that *when princes think more of luxury than of arms, they lose their state*.

Students of the modern managerial scene marvel at the total dedication of Harold Geneen, the power guiding International Telephone and Telegraph's amazing growth, to the matters of business. But Geneen is no exception. The minds of most successful businessmen seldom stray for long to extraneous matters. Business is almost their sole concern.

The average employee simply does not realize the amount of time the successful businessman spends both on the job and thinking about it.

Countless successful enterprises have gone under because their proprietors decided to forsake the office for more pleasant surroundings. A distributor of heavy construction equipment profited handsomely from his exclusive territory that included all sales to Alaska during World War II. But he grew tired of daily operations and became fonder of parties on his yacht. His liquor bill ran $6000 a month; his business suffered. The manufacturer moved in and moved him out. Today he is bankrupt.

The chief cause of the loss of states, is the contempt of this art [war], and the way to acquire them is to be well versed in the same.

Francesco Sforza, through being well armed, became, from private status, Duke of Milan; his sons, through wishing to avoid the fatigue and hardships of war, from dukes became private persons. For among other evils caused by being disarmed, it renders you contemptible; which is one of those disgraceful things which a prince must guard against, as will be explained later. Because there is no comparison whatever between an armed and a disarmed man; *it is not reasonable to suppose that one who is armed*

*will obey willingly one who is unarmed; or that any un-
armed man will remain safe among armed servants.*

What we have here is the matter of power. You cannot
reasonably expect to be obeyed unless you have the
power to enforce your own orders. Sure, some managers, because of their forceful personalities or ideals,
can maintain power over other people, but they are
exceptions. Machiavelli simply observes that it is not
reasonable to expect obedience unless one has
power, particularly when an order does not find favor
among those to whom it is given.

A department chairman harbored the delusion that
he was in charge of the professors in his department.
His consternation was continual, since his people
rarely heeded his frequent urgings and his leadership
was seldom followed. One full professor in particular
was a frequent target for the chairman's "orders":

"Don't leave early for Christmas vacation!"
"Make certain you give finals!"
"Keep your office hours!"
"Go to faculty meetings!"

As you might guess, the full professor left early,
gave no finals, kept office hours when it seemed appropriate, and seldom went to faculty meetings. Of
course, all of this infuriated the chairman—to no avail,
since he had no real power over the man. He could not
fire the professor, affect his salary, or discipline him.
The chairman continued to issue his meaningless orders to the amusement of all, not realizing the damage
it was doing to his leadership until he was eventually
driven from his job.

Lest you jump to some unwarranted conclusions,

the professor was not violating any university regulations. The chairman was merely trying to institute new
rules but he did not have the power to do so.

For one being disdainful and the other suspicious, it is
not possible for them to act well together. And therefore *a
prince who is ignorant of military matters, besides the other
misfortunes already mentioned, cannot be esteemed by his
soldiers, nor have confidence in them.*
*He ought, therefore, never to let his thoughts stray from
the exercise of war* . . .

Some years ago, a recording was widely sold which
purported to provide the listener with the true key to
success at whatever endeavor he chose to undertake.
The essence of this message was "Whatever it is you
want to do, think of nothing else: let no other thoughts
creep into your mind." Sounds good, but try it sometime. It's hard not to think forbidden thoughts. But the
principle is sound. People whose minds jump from one
thing to another seem to have difficulty operating a
business. Great men in all fields of endeavor mention
the need for concentration if one is to accomplish a job
successfully.

. . . and in peace he ought to practise it more than in
war, which he can do in two ways: by action and by study.
As to action, he must, besides keeping his men well disciplined and exercised, engage continually in hunting, and
thus accustom his body to hardships; and meanwhile learn
the nature of the land, how steep the mountains are, how
the valleys debouch, where the plains lie, and understand

the nature of rivers and swamps. To all this he should devote great attention. This knowledge is useful in two ways. In the first place, one learns to know one's country, and can the better see how to defend it. Then by means of the knowledge and experience gained in one locality, one can easily understand any other that it may be necessary to observe; for the hills and valleys, plains and rivers of Tuscany, for instance, have a certain resemblance to those of other provinces, so that from a knowledge of the country in one province one can easily arrive at a knowledge of others. And that prince who is lacking in this skill is wanting in the first essentials of a leader; for it is this which teaches how to find the enemy, take up quarters, lead armies, plan battles and lay siege to towns with advantage.

Philopoemen, prince of the Achaei, among other praises bestowed on him by writers, is lauded because in times of peace he thought of nothing but the methods of warfare, and when he was in the country with his friends, he often stopped and asked them: If the enemy were on that hill and we found ourselves here with our army, which of us would have the advantage? How could we safely approach him maintaining our order? If we wished to retire, what ought we to do? If they retired, how should we follow them? And he put before them as they went along all the contingencies that might happen to an army, heard their opinion, gave his own, fortifying it by argument; so that thanks to these constant reflections there could never happen any incident when actually leading his armies for which he was not prepared.

But as to exercise for the mind, *the prince ought to read history and study the actions of eminent men, see how they acted in warfare, examine the causes of their victories and defeats in order to imitate the former and avoid the latter . . .*

Here is the key to Machiavellian thought: Learn the nature of things by studying biographical histories. Study great men—their ways, their philosophies. Try to isolate the reasons underlying their successes and then go forth and emulate them. Study failure to understand its causation, so that you may possibly avoid the same mistakes.

The problem seems to be that seldom are we willing to study history, much less to learn from it. History clearly screams that not only will price and wage controls not work, but also that they will create a great many more problems that the ones they hope to solve. Yet in 1973 we were saddled with price controls. And in 1974 we can see their folly. History says that you can't win a war on the Asian mainland. Yet we have tried to do this twice.

History indicates that trying to compete with IBM in the large computer market is financial folly (ask General Electric, RCA, et al.), yet someone is always ready to do battle because the stakes are so attractive —seductively attractive.

But these are examples of policies, and Niccolò was concerned about the study of princes (managers). Let us take an example. What can you learn from studying Ulysses S. Grant's life—aside from the fact that fortune can cast the most unlikely people into the most unlikely roles? I have been impressed by four salient factors:

1. Grant had a *tenacity of purpose* that would have been considered a fault if he had lost. At Vicksburg and Petersburg he did not waver in his determination to win, despite opposition that had frustrated his predecessors. He simply would not be denied.

2. He forced the action—made things happen —and from the melee he forged victory as best he

could. He realized that wars cannot be won by those who are reluctant to fight.

3. He was most concerned with the abilities of his subordinates. He would not tolerate an incompetent general, and found ways to insulate his operations from their malevolent ministrations. Indeed, this may have been his real key to success: he found in Sherman, Sheridan, and Meade generals who were willing to fight and who knew how.

4. Finally, he was able to keep command over his operations by staying away from the political environment of Washington. His command was in the field and not readily accessible to visiting politicians. Abe was a lousy general. More recent presidents have had even fewer military talents, and the advent of electronic communication has allowed them to run their wars from Washington, thus insuring defeat because few politicians will do what must be done to win wars. Grant knew that war is a dirty business that requires a tenacity seldom possessed by politicians, so he took them out of the picture as best he could.

If you made a similar study of Grant, perhaps you would gain different insights into administrative behavior, but the important thing is to realize that there is much to be learned by such studies.

Admittedly, this approach to the study of management poses some problems. First, the lives of successful leaders can be contradictory: One man does one thing, another the opposite, and both are successful. So it's up to you to figure out why each method worked.

Second, it is frequently difficult to get at the truth of any matter. History is written by the victors and they usually have good reason to lie. Moreover, the truth is generally either unknown or unknowable. What is the truth in any matter? Autobiographies frequently entail little more than presenting history to the writer's advantage. Biographies range from rank character assassinations to love affairs. It is not easy to learn the ways of great men; they may not even perceive the reality of their behavior themselves.

. . . and above all, do as some men have done in the past, who have imitated some one, who has been much praised and glorified, and have always kept his deeds and actions before them, as they say Alexander the Great imitated Achilles, Caesar Alexander, and Scipio Cyrus. And whoever reads the life of Cyrus written by Xenophon, will perceive in the life of Scipio how gloriously he imitated the former, and how, in chastity, affability, humanity, and liberality Scipio conformed to those qualities of Cyrus as described by Xenophon.

A wise prince should follow similar methods and never remain idle in peaceful times, but industriously make good use of them, so that when fortune changes she may find him prepared to resist her blows, and to prevail in adversity.

Of the Things for Which Men, and Especially Princes, Are Praised or Blamed

It NOW remains to be seen what are the methods and rules for a prince as regards his subjects and friends. And as I know that many have written of this, I fear that my writing about it may be deemed presumptuous, differing as I do, especially in this matter, from the opinions of others. *But my intention being to write something of use to those who understand, it appears to me more proper to go to the real truth of the matter than to its imagination; and many have imagined republics and principalities which have never been seen or known to exist in reality; for how we live is so far removed from how we ought to live, that he who aban-*

dons what is done for what ought to be done, will rather learn to bring about his own ruin than his preservation.

Deal in reality, not wishful thinking. Niccolò had little patience with those who see people as they would like them to be rather than as they really are. This attitude may be the second key to Machiavellian philosophy.

A great deal of what has been written about management and business seems difficult to correlate with reality. One college graduate, who had been particularly enamored with the teachings of "human relations" when they first came into vogue, returned to campus and was heard to complain to his favorite professor, "You said to be honest and straightforward. Treat people with consideration and kindness. I went out, followed your directions, and got killed!"

Some material can be quite misleading. The president of one small aerospace company bragged in an industry trade journal that his company's success was due to his unique "incentive plan": "If you do your job well, you get to keep it." A few months later, the company was in financial difficulty and beset by labor troubles; that was not reported in the trade journal.

Men are prone to brag undeservedly; they twist failure into success, stupidity into brilliance. The stock trader is ready to tell you of his gains, but seldom does he disclose his losses. Situations you know intimately are unrecognizable in print. Public relations men create "boy wonders" from mediocre material; care must be taken in evaluating what one reads or hears about business.

In the summer of 1956, the president of a textile company gloated about the success of his decision to build a new textile plant in Maine rather than in the South, citing the new plant's profitability as proof. What he did not disclose was that the textile plant was no longer making textiles. Market conditions and northern wages combined to heap huge losses on the textile operation, but the Korean action had bailed him out. The textile plant operated at capacity—making machine guns—in the early 1950s. When machine guns went out of fashion so did the Maine textile plant. And so did the textile president—he was fired!

The reality behind apparent business coups usually differs from the public story.

A man who wishes to make a profession of goodness in everything must necessarily come to grief among so many who are not good.

If only Good would always triumph over Evil, but alas that is not likely to happen. Experience indicates that Good has the long odds. But why does that seem to be so? Perhaps the number of options open to each bears on the matter. Good usually must follow a narrow path with few options open to it, while Evil is left free to do whatever it believes will win the day. Thus Evil is opportunistic, exploiting every opening, while Good is usually prevented from taking advantage of such opportunities. But note that Machiavelli said, "Goodness in everything must come to grief." A man may be essentially good, but not in everything. And he may eventually triumph over Evil but still come to grief. In losing, Evil can extract a fearful price. A "good" man may have to do some "bad" things to save his enterprise, and the odds are that he *will* do them—no matter how distasteful they may be to him.

Of course, the words "good" and "bad" mean whatever your ethical base imputes to them. What is good to one man may be bad to another. Still, in our Western civilization with its Judeo-Christian ethic, there are wide areas of agreement as to what constitutes good and bad.

The fortunes of an executive—a highly esteemed pillar of the community—reversed due to some sudden market changes. Not only was his company lost, but its creditors tried to gain access to his personal wealth. He tried to protect some of his "friends" from large losses by working out various deals which would let everyone come out of the mess intact but somewhat damaged. But the creditors would not accept this; they insisted that he bear the whole burden personally, despite the legal aspects of the situation. Thus he was forced to sever many long-standing business and personal relationships that were dear to him in order to save his other enterprises which were sound but which would have been lost if he had exhausted his personal assets by continuing his virtuous behavior. The astute businessman will do what must be done to survive, to save his enterprise. If it is good, fine; if it is bad. . .

Therefore it is neccessary for a prince, who wishes to maintain himself, to learn how not to be good, and to use this knowledge and not use it, according to the necessity of the case.

Leaving on one side, then, those things which concern only an imaginary prince, and speaking of those that are real, I state that all men, and especially princes, who are placed at a greater height, are reputed for certain qualities which bring them either praise or blame. Thus one is considered liberal, another *misero* or miserly (using a Tuscan term, seeing that *avaro* with us still means one who is rapaciously acquisitive and *misero* one who makes grudging use of his own); one a free giver, another rapacious; one cruel, another merciful; one a breaker of his word, another trustworthy; one effeminate and pusillanimous, another fierce and high spirited; one humane, another haughty; one lascivious, another chaste; one frank, another astute; one hard, another easy; one serious, another frivolous; one religious, another an unbeliever, and so on. I know that every one will admit that it would be highly praiseworthy in a prince to possess all the above-named qualities that are reputed good, but as they cannot all be possessed or observed, human conditions not permitting of it, it is necessary that he should be prudent enough to avoid the scandal of those vices which would lose him the state, and guard himself if possible against those which will not lose it him, but if not able to, he can indulge them with less scruple. And yet he must not mind incurring the scandal of those vices, without which it would be difficult to save the state, for if one considers well, it will be found that some things which seem virtues would, if followed, lead to one's ruin, and some others which appear vices result in one's greater security and well-being.

Of Liberality and Niggardliness

BEGINNING now with the first qualities above named, I say that it would be well to be considered liberal; nevertheless liberality such as the world understands it will injure you, because if used virtuously and in the proper way, it will not be known, and you will incur the disgrace of the contrary vice. *But one who wishes to obtain the reputation of liberality among men, must not omit every kind of sumptuous display, and to such an extent that a prince of this character will consume by such means all his resources, and will be at last compelled, if he wishes to maintain his name for liberality, to impose heavy taxes on his people, become extortionate, and do everything possible to obtain money. This will make his subjects begin to hate him, and he will be little esteemed, being poor, so that having by this liberality injured many and benefited but few, he will feel the first little disturbance and be endangered by every peril.*

Liberality leads to dissipation of assets, which in turn either forces one to place financial demands on others which they will resent or forces one to operate more modestly.

Astute businessmen have nothing but contempt for those who dissipate their wealth frivolously, for they appreciate the value of a dollar. A "boy wonder" became president of a large corporation after some fancy financial footwork and then tried to buy the favor of the business leaders in his community. They came to his parties, drank his liquor, and accepted his lavish gifts, but when an adverse stock market placed his fortune in jeopardy, not one of them would help him. Wonder boy needed $3,000,000 to cover a margin call on a sound stock he was acquiring for strategic business purposes—$3,000,000 he would have had if not for extravagance. He was trying to take control of a very good company whose product line complemented his products nicely. He had merger in mind. Even his own directors turned their backs on him by refusing to let him use company funds, even though the venture was to benefit the company. He fled to Brazil—unwisely. Such is the fate of the spendthrift.

While a miser may not be liked, he will be respected and will retain his power. The man without resources has no power.

One businessman in a relatively small town was

obviously prospering—he had a big house and a car to match. He noted with great satisfaction that as his money began to show, people began to defer to him. He was approached by almost everyone who had some sort of a deal in mind. He got a good first look at just about all the action in town. At times, he seemed to be the economic pivot of the town. People did things for him. The road in front of his house needed repair; a phone call was all that was needed.

As his fortunes reversed, he discovered the true locus of his power—his pocketbook. He found himself excluded from the economic community, and his road now has chuckholes the year round.

If he recognises this and wishes to change his system, he incurs at once the charge of niggardliness.

A *prince*, therefore, not being able to exercise this virtue of liberality without risk if it be known, *must not, if he be prudent, object to be called miserly. In course of time he will be thought more liberal, when it is seen that by his parsimony his revenue is sufficient, that he can defend himself against those who make war on him, and undertake enterprises without burdening his people, so that he is really liberal to all those from whom he does not take, who are infinite in number, and niggardly to all to whom he does not give, who are few.*

The president of a large financial institution was bragging to one of his stockholder-directors about a large gift he had just made to a local charity. He felt he deserved some plaudits for his generosity with the company's money. His disappointment was immediate when the stockholder retorted, "And tell me

why you feel that the money is better off in their pock-
ets than mine. Why don't you give your own money
away next time?"

As Milton Friedman succinctly wrote in *An
Economist's Protest,* "Do gooders should be allowed
to do all the good they desire—with their own money."
For some reason, liberal leaders seldom realize that
their generosity to one person robs someone else.

In our times we have seen nothing great done except by
those who have been esteemed niggardly; the others have
all been ruined. Pope Julius II, although he had made use
of a reputation for liberality in order to attain the papacy,
did not seek to retain it afterwards, so that he might be able
to wage war. The present King of France has carried on so
many wars without imposing an extraordinary tax, because
his extra expenses were covered by the parsimony he had
so long practised. The present King of Spain, if he had been
thought liberal, would not have engaged in and been successful in so many enterprises.

For these reasons a prince must care little for the reputation of being a miser, if he wishes to avoid robbing his
subjects, if he wishes to be able to defend himself, to avoid
becoming poor and contemptible, and not to be forced to
become rapacious; this niggardliness is one of those vices
which enable him to reign. If it is said that Caesar attained
the empire through liberality, and that many others have
reached the highest positions through being liberal or
being thought so, I would reply that you are either a prince
already or else on the way to become one. In the first case,
this liberality is harmful; in the second, it is certainly
necessary to be considered liberal. Ceasar was one of those
who wished to attain the mastery over Rome, but if after
attaining it he had lived and had not moderated his ex-

penses, he would have destroyed that empire. And should any one reply that there have been many princes, who have done great things with their armies, who have been thought extremely liberal, I would answer by saying that the prince may either spend his own wealth and that of his subjects or the wealth of others. In the first case he must be sparing, but for the rest he must not neglect to be very liberal. The liberality is very necessary to a prince who marches with his armies, and lives by plunder, sack and ransom, and is dealing with the wealth of others, for without it he would not be followed by his soldiers. *And you may be very generous indeed with what is not the property of yourself or your subjects,* as were Cyrus, Caesar, and Alexander; *for spending the wealth of others will not diminish your reputation, but increase it; only spending your own resources will injure you.*

It would seem that most of the world's politicians have read this passage. They are generous with our money while carefully nurturing their own. And why not? Robbing the rich is a popular doctrine to the masses.

There is nothing which destroys itself so much as liberality, for by using it you lose the power of using it, and become either poor and despicable, or, to escape poverty, rapacious and hated. And of all things that a prince must guard against, the most important are being despicable or hated, and liberality will lead you to one or the other of these conditions. It is, therefore, wiser to have the name of a miser, which produces disgrace without hatred, than to incur of necessity the name of being rapacious, which produces both disgrace and hatred.

Of Cruelty and Clemency, and Whether It Is Better to Be Loved or Feared

PROCEEDING to the other qualities before named, I say that every prince must desire to be considered merciful and not cruel. He must, however, take care not to misuse this mercifulness. Cesare Borgia was considered cruel, but his cruelty had brought order to the Romagna, united it, and reduced it to peace and fealty. If this is considered well, it will be seen that he was really much more merciful than the Florentine people, who, to avoid the name of cruelty, allowed Pistoia to be destroyed. A prince, therefore, must not mind incurring the charge of cruelty for the purpose of keeping his subjects united and faithful; for,

75

with a very few examples, he will be more merciful than those who, from excess of tenderness, allow disorders to arise, from whence spring bloodshed and rapine; for these as a rule injure the whole community, while the executions carried out by the prince injure only individuals. *And of all princes, it is impossible for a new prince to escape the reputation of cruelty, new states being always full of dangers.*

> New administrators had better ponder these words, for they provide a bitter lesson that will soon become painfully apparent. In some situations the new manager will be forced to behave in a manner that many people will consider cruel. Should he shy away from taking needed actions to avoid seeming cruel, continued organizational deviations will eventually either cause him greater difficulty or force him to commit the cruelties he was hoping to avoid.

Wherefore Virgil, through the mouth of Dido, says:
  Res dura, et regni novitas me talia cogunt
  Moliri, et late fines custode tueri.
Nevertheless, he must be cautious in believing and acting, and must not be afraid of his own shadow, and must proceed in a temperate manner with prudence and humanity, so that too much confidence does not render him incautious, and too much diffidence does not render him intolerant.

From this arises the question whether it is better to be loved more than feared, or feared more than loved. *The reply is, that one ought to be both feared and loved, but as it is difficult for the two to go together, it is much safer to be feared than loved . . .*

A Big Ten university once hired a fine football coach. He was truly loved by his players and his colleagues. He was a wonderful person, but his team did not win. It did not even make a good showing, although his coaching was technically sound. His players couldn't hit hard enough to hurt. They were soft. The coach lasted two seasons.

On the other hand, Vince Lombardi was feared. He came to be loved, but first he was feared. Yet his men hit, and his men won!

What about businessmen? Managers? Should they seek appreciation? Many do, to their eventual disillusionment. It is only natural for a man to want the respect of his fellow workers, his peers, his subordinates, and—yes—his boss. But the question is, "What price does he have to pay to get it?" The answer to this is often "loss of control."

Mike, a successful young salesman who was well liked by his peers, was promoted to sales manager when his predecessor—who had not been popular, despite his performance record—resigned. Mike was determined to be close to his men, to be their friend. He ran a happy ship. "Good place to work!" "He's a great guy!" "Easy going." "Everybody likes him." Such comments were frequent.

But the big boss began to notice the results: both sales and profits were down. He asked Mike for a report on the matter and was given some noise about "market conditions" that did not quite square with his concept of reality. The boss also noticed that sales expenses were up and had asked to see the salesmen's call reports for the previous month. Many were missing; most that were there were not records of inspired performances, to say the least. So he had an assistant make a quiet investigation. His report revealed Mike's lax managment. The salesmen's work habits had degenerated. The men simply were not working hard; they started late, quit early, and took long coffee breaks.

The boss called Mike in and the two men spent a great deal of time discussing managerial philosophies after Mike declared that he was aware of his men's seemingly lax work habits but that was the way he wanted to manage. Mike went on to point out that not one man had quit during his reign. Moreover, he maintained, the company would be better off in the long run with a happy sales force.

The boss pulled out the most recent expense account of one salesman. It was so obviously padded that Mike had to restrain a wince upon hearing: "Please explain how this is to the company's long-term advantage!"

"That's Jim. Now there are some extenuating circumstances behind that that you don't know about. He's having a hard time financially. He's pressing for every buck," Mike explained.

"So I'm supposed to foot his bills, is that it?"

Mike's answer was oblique,"He'll get this problem whipped, and when it's over we'll have a man even more loyal to us than before. If I call him on the carpet or disapprove some of his expenses, we'll lose his good will."

"What about my good will?" the boss had asked.

From the ensuing discussion Mike promised to take a firmer hand with his men, to shape them up. He sensed his job depended upon this, and the next few months saw a change in his managerial behavior. Expense accounts were questioned, men were given definite work quotas, a few were disciplined, and one was fired. The dismissal erupted suddenly during a meeting with a salesman whose call reports strayed from the truth.

At the end of three months, sales were up and

expenses were down—but the company now had one disillusioned sales manager. Mike discovered that his "friends" did not react kindly to his new style of leadership. "Got the big head!" "Playing like a big shot!" "I thought he was a regular guy!" could now be heard. Mike soon realized that he was held in contempt by his ex-friends, while his predecessor—who had been regarded as a "tough" boss—was still respected, although he had been feared.

. . . if one of the two has to be wanting. For it may be said of men in general that they are ungrateful, voluble, dissemblers, anxious to avoid danger, and covetous of gain; as long as you benefit them, they are entirely yours; they offer you their blood, their goods, their life, and their children, as I have before said, when the necessity is remote, but when it approaches, they revolt. And the prince who has relied solely on their words, without making other preparations, is ruined; for the friendship which is gained by purchase and not through grandeur and nobility of spirit is bought but not secured, and at a pinch is not to be expended in your service. *And men have less scruple in offending one who makes himself loved than one who makes himself feared; for love is held by a chain of obligation which, men being selfish, is broken whenever it serves their purpose; but fear is maintained by a dread of punishment which never fails.*

Admittedly, this particular passage has been subject to much criticism, for it appalls certain people who do not care to see its logic and truthfulness. A vote against love and in favor of fear is not calculated to win

plaudits, but in numerous cases people have sac-
rificed loved ones out of fear for themselves, contrary
to our cultural standard.

Think a bit. You have a right to expect a person you
love to be more than tolerant of your faults. Friends
must accept each other as they are—faults and all.
That is one of the beauties of friendship: You don't
have to try to be something you aren't. You can just be
yourself and your friends will accept you. So a manager who rules by friendship must be prepared to
accept his men more or less as they are. Friends do
not remain friends for long when one is trying to reform
the other.

On the other hand, a man who is not a friend but who
controls something you want is somewhat feared. You
are likely to behave as you think he wants you to
behave so that he will give you what you want. A friend
would give it to you without such behavior.

*Still a prince should make himself feared in such a way
that if he does not gain love, he at any rate avoids hatred;
for fear and the absence of hatred may well go together,
and will be always attained by one who abstains from
interfering with the property of his citizens and
subjects. . .*

Evidently it is difficult for some people to distinguish
between fear and hatred, for I have heard arguments
that people hate those they fear. Perhaps, but not
necessarily! Love can also be a handmaiden of fear.
Fear of another person is the emotion generated when
one is apprehensive about what may happen to him
should he do something that displeases that person.
There are people who fear, yet still love, their spouses.

Hatred, on the other hand, is the emotion generated when one person dislikes another so strongly that he would harm him if given the opportunity. You can fear someone, yet not want harm to befall him.

And when he is *obliged to take the life of anyone, let him do so when there is a proper justification and manifest reason for it; but above all he must abstain from taking the property of others, for men forget more easily the death of their father than the loss of their patrimony.*

Managers must not only respect the property of others, but they must also administer punishment justly. A man punished unfairly will develop a hatred that may drive him to seek revenge. Thus, it may be far wiser to fire a worker than to discipline him severely. The person who has been disciplined may wait for an opportunity to avenge himself—an opportunity that usually occurs sooner or later.

Then also *pretexts for seizing property are never wanting. . .*

A person will find a reason for doing whatever mischief he is of a mind to do. Two men in a profitable partnership began arguing over a number of issues. Feelings became bitter on both sides. While their agreement provided for the return of the minority partner's capital ($40,000) should the partnership be dissolved, that's not the way it worked. By a series of rather clever legal maneuvers, the controlling partner managed to seize

his adversary's property. Almost without exception, when business associates disagree, their thoughts are to "grab the money and run." The man in control of the property holds the upper hand, for the courts are imperfect mechanisms for righting such wrongs. And such men are always so righteous in defense of their skullduggery.

. . . and one who begins to live by rapine will always find some reason for taking the goods of others, whereas causes for taking life are rarer and more fleeting.

But when the prince is with his army and has a large number of soldiers under his control, then it is extremely necessary that he should not mind being thought cruel; for without this reputation he could not keep an army united or disposed to any duty. Among the noteworthy actions of Hannibal is numbered this, that although he had an enormous army, composed of men of all nations and fighting in foreign countries, there never arose any dissension either among them or against the prince, either in good fortune or in bad. This could not be due to anything but his inhuman cruelty, which together with his infinite other virtues, made him always venerated and terrible in the sight of his soldiers, and without it his other virtues would not have sufficed to produce the effect. Thoughtless writers admire on the one hand his actions, and on the other blame the principal cause of them.

And that it is true that his other virtues would not have sufficed may be seen from the case of Scipio (famous not only in regard to his own times, but all times of which memory remains), whose armies rebelled against him in Spain, which arose from nothing but his excessive kindness, which allowed more licence to the soldiers than was consonant with military discipline. He was reproached with this in the senate by Fabius Maximus, who called him a corrupter of the Roman militia. Lorcri having been destroyed by one of Scipio's officers was not revenged by him, nor was the insolence of that officer punished, simply by reason of his easy nature; so much so, that some one wishing to excuse him in the senate, said that there were many men who knew rather how not to err, than how to correct the errors of others. This disposition would in time have tarnished the fame and glory of Scipio had he persevered in it under the empire, but living under the rule of the senate, this harmful quality was not only concealed but became a glory to him.

I conclude, therefore, with regard to being feared and loved, that men love at their own free will, but fear at the will of the prince, and that a wise prince must rely on what is in his power and not on what is in the power of others, and he must only contrive to avoid incurring hatred, as has been explained.

In What Way Princes Must Keep Faith

HOW LAUDABLE it is for a prince to keep good faith and live with integrity, and not with astuteness, every one knows. *Still the experience of our times shows those princes to have done great things who have had little regard for good faith, and have been able by astuteness to confuse men's brains, and who have ultimately overcome those who have made loyalty their foundation.*

This is one of Machiavelli's major points: Contrary to what one might like to believe, leaders *do not have to keep faith* or keep their word. Disguises for breaking faith are seldom lacking. For years, the United States steadfastly maintained that, come what may, it would hold the price of gold at $35 an ounce, allowing the world to sleep well at night with its wealth in dollars. As our economic policies made that gold price less and less feasible, the U.S. government still tried to convince the naive that the $35 price was inviolate, but sophisticates knew better. They fled from dollars to gold, thus compounding Uncle Sam's problem. Finally faith was broken, and for good reason—it always is for a good reason.

Bear in mind that persons betrayed by a leader's lack of faith are seldom in a position to do anything about it. Indeed, they may find it more comfortable to accept the leader's excuse for betrayal because they realize that they have no viable alternative to his leadership. Those who reject their leader's rationale for betrayal usually have trouble continuing to relate to that leader. Many times the individual realizes that he needs to maintain that relationship, so betrayal be damned.

To carry his small manufacturing company through a difficult time, the president broke faith with his employees by borrowing money from their pension fund, managed by the company's officers in cooperation with a few trusted employees, despite written provisions not to do so. But what could the trustees do? Refuse, and the company fails—or so it appeared. Then where would they all be? Only a foolish manager would allow his organization to fail simply to keep a previous promise.

You must know, then, that there are two methods of fighting, the one by law, the other by force: the first method is that of men, the second of beasts; but as the first method is often insufficient, one must have recourse to the second.

> Precisely the situation encountered by the unions in their struggle for existence. When the law proved inadequate, they resorted to force; then the law slowly came around.
>
> Various minority groups are presently discovering the true role of force in the affairs of man. Ultimate power is the result of ultimate force. Realize that one need not use force if the adversary believes that force may be used. The existence of potential force is all that is usually necessary. This has been the basis of U.S. foreign policy since World War II: Possess force and show that you are willing to use it when necessary.

It is therefore necessary for a prince to know well how to use both the beast and the man. This was covertly taught to rulers by ancient writers, who relate how Achilles and many others of those ancient princes were given to Chiron the centaur to be brought up and educated under his discipline. The parable of this semi-animal, semi-human teacher is meant to indicate that a prince must know how to use both natures, and that the one without the other is not durable.

A prince being thus obliged to know well how to act as a beast must imitate the fox and the lion, for the lion cannot protect himself from traps, and the fox cannot defend himself from wolves. One must therefore be a fox to recognise traps, and a lion to frighten wolves. Those that wish to be only lions do not understand this. *Therefore, a prudent ruler ought not to keep faith when by so doing it would be*

against his interest, and when the reasons which made him
bind himself no longer exist.

This passage disturbs many people who wish it were
otherwise, but its truth is apparent to most.

Promises—unless their fulfillment is currently
advantageous—mean little to the executive. His mind
can perform amazing acrobatics to rationalize its behavior.

Two men—let's call them Paul and Max—were the
closest of friends. They were buddies in high school, in
college, in the army, and then went into business together. Paul had a bit more money to put into the
business so he ended up with a little more stock. All
went well; the enterprise prospered. As the stakes
grew larger, Paul's interest in sharing them shrank
commensurately. He really did not need Max to run the
business, so Paul began to notice little faults in Max
which had always been there but had never been of
any consequence before. Paul's mind magnified
Max's inadequacies until they overwhelmed him. Max
was out. All promises were broken.

It is imprudent to rely on unenforceable promises in
the affairs of men. However, there are times when one
has no practical alternative but to rely upon some
promise. Just don't bank on it being carried out. Don't
allow your fortunes to depend upon some promise that
may or may not be kept unless, of course, you have no
option.

If men were all good, this precept would not be a good
one; but as they are bad, and would not observe their faith
with you, so you are not bound to keep faith with them.
Nor have legitimate grounds ever failed a prince who
wished to show colourable excuse for the non-fulfilment of

his promise. Of this one could furnish an infinite number of modern examples, and show how many times peace has been broken, and how many promises rendered worthless, by the faithlessness of princes, and those that have been best able to imitate the fox have succeeded best. But it is necessary to be able to disguise this character well, and to be a great feigner and dissembler; and *men are so simple and so ready to obey present necessities, that one who deceives will always find those who allow themselves to be deceived.*

And this is what allows a leader to deceive: Others in the organization are so simple or naive that they unprotestingly swallow the lies fed to them. The business scene continually provides us with examples of glib-tongued rascals who create financial empires from paper and promises. The thousands of people who lose money when such swindles are exposed wonder how they could have believed such tales; many of those who were duped refuse to admit it to protect their egos from the harsh conclusion that they are simple fools.

People believe deceptions because they want to believe them. It is easier for them to believe than to disbelieve, for disbelief would present them with an uncomfortable dilemma: whether to keep silent in the face of an injustice or to take some action that might be risky.

People believe a swindler's lies because they are greedy. They want to believe that the man is going to make them rich.

I will only mention one modern instance. Alexander VI did nothing else but deceive men; he thought of nothing else, and found the occasion for it; no man was ever more able to give assurances, or affirmed things with stronger oaths, and no man observed them less; however, he always succeeded in his deceptions, as he well knew this aspect of things.

It is not, therefore, necessary for a prince to have all the above-named qualities, but it is very necessary to seem to have them. I would even be bold to say that to possess them and always to observe them is dangerous, but to appear to possess them is useful. *Thus it is well to seem merciful, faithful, humane, sincere, religious, and also to be so; but you must have the mind so disposed that when it is needful to be otherwise you may be able to change to the opposite qualities.*

Ah, yes, the platform of politicians and many administrators. Appearances are not only important but also deceiving. The problem is that we seldom have much of anything else upon which to base our judgments of people, so appearances must do. We accept what appearances suggest unless we possess information to the contrary.

And it must be understood that a prince, and especially a new prince, cannot observe all those things which are considered good in men, being often obliged, in order to maintain the state, to act against faith, against charity, against humanity, and against religion. *And, therefore, he must have a mind disposed to adapt itself according to the wind, and as the variations of fortune dictate, and, as I said before, not deviate from what is good, if possible, but be able to do evil if constrained.*

A policy of expediency: Do what the situation demands! The statement seized by Machiavelli's critics
in condemning his work! But read it in its context.
Niccolò is saying: Do good whenever you can, but
don't be afraid to do evil if the need arises.

Outstanding performance throws a cloak of protection over the administrator's tactics. But be warned:
Don't take this as a license to do whatever one wishes.
There are always limits beyond which trouble lies for
any administrator, no matter what his record might be.

Recall the firing of a bright, able president of a television network who had proved he had the ability to
develop highly successful television programs. Subsequent disclosures indicated that he had been discharged because his superiors felt that many personal
aspects of his behavior were unacceptable. His outstanding record was insufficient to justify his personal
excesses.

A prince must take great care that nothing goes out of his
mouth which is not full of the above-named five qualities,
and, to see and hear him, he should seem to be all mercy,
faith, integrity, humanity, and religion. And nothing is
more necessary than to seem to have this last quality, for
men in general judge more by the eyes than by the hands,
for everyone can see, but very few have to feel. Everybody
sees what you appear to be, few feel what you are, and
those few will not dare to oppose themselves to the many,
who have the majesty of the state to defend them; and in
the actions of men, and especially of princes, from which
there is no appeal, the end justifies the means. Let a prince
therefore aim at conquering and maintaining the state, and
the means will always be judged honourable and praised by
everyone, for the vulgar is always taken by appearances

and the issue of the event; and the world consists only of the vulgar, and the few who are not vulgar are isolated when the many have a rallying point in the prince. A certain prince of the present time, whom it is well not to name, never does anything but preach peace and good faith, but he is really a great enemy to both, and either of them, had he observed them, would have lost him state or reputation on many occasions.

That We Must Avoid Being Despised and Hated

BUT AS I have now spoken of the most important of the qualities in question, I will now deal briefly and generally with the rest. The prince must, as already stated, avoid those things which will make him hated or despised; and whenever he succeeds in this, he will have done his part, and will find no danger in other vices. He will chiefly become hated, as I said, by being rapacious, and usurping the property and women of his subjects, which he must abstain from doing, and whenever one does not attack the property or honour of the generality of men, they will live contented; and one will only have to combat the ambition of a few, who can be easily held in check in many ways. *He is rendered despicable by being thought changeable, frivolous, effeminate, timid, and irresolute...*

Take note of these traits. Is the message that a leader must play the role of the big, strong he-man? Does this partly explain all the polar bear and elk heads mounted in executive suites?

... which a prince must guard against as a rock of danger, and so contrive that his actions show grandeur, spirit, gravity, and fortitude; and as to the government of his subjects, let his sentence be irrevocable, and let him adhere to his decisions so that no one may think of deceiving or cozening him.

The prince who creates such an opinion of himself gets a great reputation, and it is very difficult to conspire against one who has a great reputation, and he will not easily be attacked, so long as it is known that he is capable and reverenced by his subjects. For a prince must have two kinds of fear: one internal as regards his subjects, one external as regards foreign powers. From the latter he can defend himself with good arms and good friends, and he will always have good friends if he has good arms; and internal matters will always remain quiet, if they are not perturbed by conspiracy and there is no disturbance from without; and even if external powers sought to attack him, if he has ruled and lived as I have described, he will always, if he stands firm, be able to sustain every shock, as I have shown that Nabis the Spartan did. But with regard to the subjects, if not acted on from outside, it is still to be feared lest they conspire in secret, from which the prince may guard himself well by avoiding hatred and contempt, and keeping the people satisfied with him, which it is necessary to accomplish, as has been related at length. And one of the most potent remedies that a prince has against conspiracies, is that of not being hated by the mass of the people; for whoever conspires always believes that he will satisfy the people by the death of their prince; but if he thought to offend them by doing this, he would fear to engage in such an undertaking, for the difficulties that conspirators have to meet are infinite. *Experience shows that there have been very many conspiracies, but few have turned out well, for whoever conspires cannot act alone, and cannot find companions except among those who are discontented; and as soon as you have disclosed your intention to a malcontent, you give him the means of satisfying himself, for by revealing it he can hope to secure everything he wants . . .*

Conspiracies are hazardous ventures. A college administrator managed to get his group into academic hot water by not being attentive to the details of running his office. He announced his failure to his people and asked to be relieved of his responsibilities, but he was so popular that they gave him a vote of confidence. He had many fine qualities; paper work unfortunately wasn't one of them.

However, six of his subordinates discussed the situation and, for several reasons they felt were good, decided not only that it would be best to have new leadership but that it would be the kindest thing they could do for their boss. They decided to put two men into the office to clean up the mess—one to handle the inside problems and the other to handle those outside. They devised a plan to contact everyone in the organization individually. Each man was to invite certain people to an informal meeting where the final plans would be developed. The meeting turned into another vote of confidence, as everyone was "forced" by a few well-meaning, emotional friends of the leader to sign a petition to top management reaffirming the organization's faith in him. Such was this man's hold on his people.

But it was all to no avail. The big boss summarily dismissed the man because he was unable to do the job. But the conspirators suffered greatly at the hands of their old "friends" in the organization. The wounds never healed; things were never the same again. A wise man stays clear of such conspiracies; there is not much to be gained and there is much to lose.

. . . to such an extent that seeing a certain gain by doing this, and seeing on the other hand only a doubtful one and full of danger, he must either be a rare friend to you or else a very bitter enemy to the prince if he keeps faith with you. And to express the matter in a few words, I say, that *on the side of the conspirator there is nothing but fear, jealousy, suspicion, and dread of punishment which frightens him; and on the side of the prince there is the majesty of government, the laws, the protection of friends and of the state which guard him.* When to these things is added the good will of the people, it is impossible that anyone should have the temerity to conspire. For whereas generally *a conspirator has to fear before the execution of his plot, in this case, having the people for an enemy, he must also fear after his crime is accomplished, and thus he is not able to hope for any refuge.*

In another academic situation (peculiar that our examples of conspiracy are centered in the academic world), four of the senior department heads in a college were distressed about a new dean's plans for them. The dean thought little of their talents, and rightly so. They conspired! As a group, they walked into the president's office with a list of grievances—there are always grievances—to demand the dean's dismissal.

Not only did the president listen to them, but he bought their story without hearing the other side. He pressured the dean into a short stay—only a bit shorter than his own. However, the conspirators reaped not plaudits for their success, but scorn. They had destroyed themselves. Never again were they given any power in the organization. They were practically ostracized. The next dean removed them from their positions of power. How could he trust the rascals? History deals harshly with conspirators.

Numberless instances might be given of this, but I will content myself with one which took place within the memory of our fathers. Messer Annibale Bentivogli, Prince of Bologna, ancestor of the present Messer Annibale, was killed by the Canneschi, who conspired against him. He left no relations but Messer Giovanni, who was then an infant, but after the murder the people rose up and killed all the Canneschi. This arose from the popular good will that the house of Bentivogli enjoyed at that time, which was so great that, as there was nobody left after the death of Annibale who could govern the state, the Bolognese hearing that there was one of the Bentivogli family in Florence, who had till then been thought the son of a blacksmith, came to fetch him and gave him the government of the city, and it was governed by him until Messer Giovanni was old enough to assume the government.

I conclude, therefore, that a prince need trouble little about conspiracies when the people are well disposed, but when they are hostile and hold him in hatred, then he must fear everything and everybody. Well-ordered states and wise princes have studied diligently not to drive the nobles to desperation, and to satisfy the populace and keep it contented, for this is one of the most important matters that a prince has to deal with.

Whence it may be seen that hatred is gained as much by good works as by evil, and therefore, as I said before, a prince who wishes to maintain the state is often forced to do evil, for when that party, whether populace, soldiery, or nobles, whichever it be that you consider necessary to you for keeping your position, is corrupt, you must follow its humour and satisfy it, and in that case good works will be inimical to you. But let us come to Alexander, who was of such goodness, that among other things for which he is praised, it is said that in the fourteen years that he reigned no one was put to death by him without a fair trial. Nevertheless, being considered effeminate, and a man who allowed himself to be ruled by his mother, and having thus fallen into contempt, the army conspired against him and killed him.

Considering, on the other hand, the qualities of Commodus, Severus, Antoninus, Caracalla, and Maximinus, you will find them extremely cruel and rapacious; to satisfy the soldiers there was no injury which they would not inflict on the people, and all except Severus ended badly. Severus, however, had such abilities that by maintaining the soldiers' friend [ship] . . . he was able to reign happily, although he oppressed the people, for his virtues made him so admirable in the sight both of the soldiers and the people that the latter were, in some degree, astonished and stupefied, while the former were respectful and contented.

As the deeds of this ruler were great and notable for a new prince, I will briefly show how well he could use the qualities of the fox and the lion, whose natures, as I said before, it is necessary for a prince to imitate. Knowing the sloth of the Emperor Julianus, Severus, who was leader of the army in Slavonia, persuaded the troops that it would be well to go to Rome to avenge the death of Pertinax, who had been slain by the Praetorian guard, and under this pretext, without revealing his aspirations to the throne, marched with his army to Rome and was in Italy before his departure was known. On his arrival in Rome the senate elected him emperor through fear, and killed Julianus. There remained after this beginning two difficulties to be faced by Severus before he could obtain the whole control of the empire: one in Asia, where Nigrinus, head of the Asiatic armies, had declared himself emperor; the other in the west from Albinus, who also aspired to the empire. *And as he judged it dangerous to show himself hostile to both, he decided to attack Nigrinus and deceive Albinus . . .*

And the well-recognized tactic—divide and conquer —is introduced. The word "conquer" seems to bother some purists. Perhaps they would feel better if we termed the tactic "divide and keep from being conquered." No matter! The point is that there are a great many instances in which the wise manager will take pains to insure that potential adversaries do not join forces against him. To do otherwise would be foolish.

And when one is faced with several united foes, what is the wisdom of fighting them together? Rare is the alliance of adversaries who leave no internal conflicts of interest which can be used to divide them. Conversion of a foe into an ally is not necessary for this tactic to be successful; the neutralization or even the slackening of a foe's desire to do battle may be all that is needed to win the day.

As Machiavelli indicates, frequently the administrator must deceive one of his foes to break down a consolidated adversary. A new branch manager for a large Wall Street brokerage detected that three of his best account executives were forming a coalition to oppose some new work rules he had instituted. He singled out the best man, invited him to lunch, and hinted that he had heard in the home office that a promotion might be in the offing for the man. Sensing that participation in a confrontation with the branch manager would do little to further his future in the company, the man decided to pull in his horns. The other two men wisely decided to abandon their plans when their forces were so severely weakened. By the time the rebel realized the hint was false, it was too late for him to mount an attack.

. . . to whom [Albinus] he [Severus] wrote that having been elected emperor by the senate he wished to share that dignity with him; he sent him the title of Caesar and, by deliberation of the senate, he was declared his colleague; all of which was accepted as true by Albinus. But when Severus had defeated and killed Nigrinus, and pacified things in the East, he returned to Rome and charged Albinus in the senate with having, unmindful of the benefits received from him, traitorously sought to assassinate him, and stated that he was therefore obliged to go and punish his ingratitude. He then went to France to meet him, and there deprived him of both his position and his life.

Whoever examines in detail the actions of Severus, will find him to have been a very ferocious lion and an extremely astute fox and will find him to have been feared and respected by all and not hated by the army; and will not be surprised that he, a new man, should have been able to hold so much power, since his great reputation defended him always from the hatred that his rapacity might have produced in the people. But Antoninus his son was also a man of great ability, and possessed qualities that rendered him admirable in the sight of the people and also made him popular with the soldiers, for he was a military man, capable of enduring the most extreme hardships, disdainful of delicate food, and every other luxury, which made him loved by all the armies. However, his ferocity and cruelty were so great and unheard of, through his having, after executing many private individuals, caused a large part of the population of Rome and all that of Alexandria to be killed, that he became hated by all the world and began to be feared by those about him to such an extent that he was finally killed by a centurion in the midst of his army. Whence it is to be noted that this kind of death, which proceeds from the deliberate action of a determined man, cannot be avoided by princes, since any one who does not fear death himself can inflict it, but a prince need not fear much on this account, as such men are extremely rare. *He must only guard against committing any grave injury to any one he makes use of, or has about him for his service. . . .*

One tyrant who called himself a businessman took sadistic glee in verbally lashing his employees at every opportunity (and he found many). He went out of his way to torment the help. Naturally, few men would work for him, but those who did extracted their revenge—daily. "Embezzlement" is the legal term; "tapping the till" is the jargon. The tyrant had welded his employees into a cohesive group of people who hated him enough to steal from him, for his control systems relied upon the employees keeping each other honest.

Don't keep an employee around after you have harmed him. Forgiveness is not a human virtue upon which one can rely.

. . . like Antoninus had done, having caused the death with contumely of the brother of that centurion, and also threatened him every day, although he still retained him in his bodyguard, which was a foolish and dangerous thing to do, as the fact proved.

But let us come to Commodus, who might easily have kept the empire, having succeeded to it by heredity, being the son of Marcus, and it would have sufficed for him to follow in the steps of his father to have satisfied both the people and the soldiers. But being of a cruel and bestial disposition, in order to be able to exercise his rapacity on the people, he sought to favour the soldiers and render them licentious; on the other hand, by not maintaining his dignity, by often descending into the theatre to fight with gladiators and committing other contemptible actions little worthy of the imperial dignity, he became despicable in the eyes of the soldiers, and being hated on the one hand and despised on the other, he was conspired against and killed.

There remains to be described the character of Maximinus. He was an extremely warlike man, and as the armies were annoyed with the effeminacy of Alexander . . . he was elected emperor after the death of the latter. He did not enjoy it for long, as two things made him hated and

despised: the one his base origin, as he had been a shep-
herd in Thrace, which was generally known and caused
great disdain on all sides; the other, because he had at the
commencement of his rule deferred going to Rome to take
possession of the Imperial seat, and had obtained a reputation for great cruelty, having through his prefects in Rome
and other parts of the empire committed many acts of
cruelty. The whole world being thus moved by indignation
for the baseness of his blood, and also by the hatred caused
by fear of his ferocity, he was conspired against first by
Africa and afterwards by the senate and all the people of
Rome and Italy. His own army also joined them, for besieging Aquileia and finding it difficult to take, they became
enraged at his cruelty, and seeing that he had so many
enemies, they feared him less and put him to death.

I will not speak of Heliogabalus, of Macrinus, or
Julianus, who being entirely contemptible were immediately suppressed, but I will come to the conclusion of this
discourse by saying that the princes of our time have less
difficulty than these in being obliged to satisfy in an extraordinary degree their soldiers in their states; for although
they must have a certain consideration for them, yet any
difficulty is soon settled, for none of these princes have
armies that are inextricably bound up with the administration of the government and the rule of their provinces as
were the armies of the Roman empire. If it was then
necessary to satisfy the soldiers rather than the people, it
was because the soldiers could do more than the people;
now, it is more necessary for all princes, except the Turk
and the Sultan, to satisfy the people than the soldiers, for
the people can do more than the soldiers. I except the
Turk, because he always keeps about him twelve thousand
infantry and fifteen thousand cavalry, on which depend the
security and strength of his kingdom; and it is necessary for

him to postpone every other consideration to keep them friendly. It is the same with the kingdom of the Sultan, which being entirely in the hands of the soldiers, he is bound to keep their friendship, regardless of the people. And it is to be noted that this state of the Sultan is different from that of all other princes, being similar to the Christian pontificate, which cannot be called either a hereditary kingdom or a new one, for the sons of the dead prince are not his heirs, but he who is elected to that position by those who have authority. And as this order is ancient it cannot be called a new kingdom, there being none of these difficulties which exist in new ones; as although the prince is new, the rules of that state are old and arranged to receive him as if he were their hereditary lord.

But returning to our matter, I say that whoever studies the preceding argument will see that either hatred or contempt were the causes of the ruin of the emperors named, and will also observe how it came about that, some of them acting in one way and some in another, in both ways there were some who had a fortunate and others an unfortunate ending. As Pertinax and Alexander were both new rulers, it was useless and injurious for them to try and imitate Marcus, who was a hereditary prince; and similarly with Caracalla, Commodus, and Maximinus it was pernicious for them to imitate Severus, as they had not sufficient ability to follow in his footsteps. Thus a new prince cannot imitate the actions of Marcus, in his dominions, nor is it necessary for him to imitate those of Severus; but he must take from Severus those things that are necessary to found his state, and from Marcus those that are useful and glorious for conserving a state that is already established and secure.

How Flatterers
Must Be Shunned

I MUST NOT omit an important subject, and mention of a
mistake which princes can with difficulty avoid, if they are
not very prudent, or if they do not make a good choice. And
this is with regard to flatterers, of which courts are full,
because men take such pleasure in their own things and
deceive themselves about them that they can with
difficulty guard against this plague; and by wishing to guard
against it, they run the risk of becoming contemptible.
Because there is no other way of guarding one's self against
flattery than by letting men understand that they will not
offend you by speaking the truth; but when everyone can

tell you the truth, you lose their respect. A prudent prince must therefore take a third course by choosing for his council wise men and giving these alone full liberty to speak the truth to him, but only of those things that he asks and of nothing else . . .

A rapidly rising corporate executive was on what the younger generation calls "an ego trip." He held a rather healthy regard for his own opinions, and his subordinates quickly perceived that any voice contrary to the boss would be dealt with harshly. Thus the man heard only the noises that he wanted to hear. One of his pet programs was a real bomb. Everyone in the organization knew that it was going to lose a great deal of money, but each steadfastly affirmed to the boss that his program was sheer genius. The executive was fired when large losses made the truth apparent. If you won't tolerate the truth, then you'll dine on lies. If you wish to hear the truth, you must select your counselors carefully.

Dave was a manufacturer of custom-made bikinis. One woman employee in the shop possessed unusually good judgment about most things, and the opinions of a bright young man in sales had proved to be sound. Dave often directed specific questions to these two people. He would listen to their advice without argument, without comment, always indicating his appreciation for their thoughts. Then when he was alone he would digest their thoughts and combine them with his own to arrive at a decision. Dave felt the system worked well for him. He was pleased with the quality of the advice he was given.

Clearly, there is an art to seeking advice from other people and still keeping control of the relationship. The administrator should ask straightforward questions about specific problems. While he should not engage in debate, he can probe more deeply into a subject by asking questions. People who render opinions outside their area of competence should be shunned, but unfortunately they seldom are. So-called experts in one field of endeavor often seem bent on forcing their opinions in another area—whether or not they know much about it—on anyone naive enough to listen.

The president of one electronics manufacturing concern was unable to keep a marketing executive for long because he continually used his engineer's opinions to refute the marketing expert's plans.

An administrator should not accept general, broad-scale opinions—either pro or con. Rather, he should require that the advisor be specific. The opinions of those prone to talking in generalities are of little value.

. . . but he must ask them about everything and hear their opinion, and afterwards deliberate by himself in his own way, and in these councils and with each of these men comport himself so that everyone may see that the more freely he speaks, the more he will be acceptable. Beyond these he should listen to no one, go about the matter deliberately, and be determined in his decisions. Whoever acts otherwise either acts precipitately through flattery or else changes often through the variety of opinions, from which it follows that he will be little esteemed.

History indicates that Queen Elizabeth I so used her Privy Council. She would listen patiently to each member's argument, but would make her own decision at the place and time she chose. It was said that no one ever really knew what she was thinking or what plan she was following. Considering the perils of the

times and her position and in view of her success, she
must rate as one of the greatest tacticians of all time.

I will give a modern instance of this. Pre' Luca, a follower of Maximilian, the present emperor, speaking of his
majesty said that he never took counsel with anybody, and
yet that he never did anything as he wished; this arose from
his following the contrary method to the aforesaid. As the
emperor is a secret man he does not communicate his
designs to anyone or take any advice, but as on putting
them into effect they begin to be known and discovered,
they begin to be opposed by those he has about him, and he
is easily diverted from his purpose. Hence it comes to pass
that what he does one day he undoes the next, no one ever
understands what he wishes or intends to do, and no
reliance is to be placed on his deliberations.

*A prince, therefore, ought always to take counsel, but
only when he wishes, not when others wish; on the contrary
he ought to discourage absolutely attempts to advise him
unless he asks it, but he ought to be a great asker,* and a
patient hearer of the truth about those things of which he
has inquired; indeed, if he finds that anyone has scruples in
telling him the truth, he should be angry. And since some
think that a prince who gains the reputation of being prudent is so considered, not by his nature but by the good
counsellors he has about him, they are undoubtedly deceived. It is an infallible rule that a prince who is not wise
himself cannot be well advised, unless by chance he leaves
himself entirely in the hands of one man who rules him in
everything, but happens to be a very prudent man. In this
case he may doubtless be well governed, but it would not
last long, for that governor would in a short time deprive
him of the state; but by taking counsel with many, a prince

who is not wise will never have united councils and will not be able to bring them to unanimity for himself. The counsellors will all think of their own interests, and he will be unable either to correct or to understand them. *And it cannot be otherwise, for men will always be false to you unless they are compelled by necessity to be true.*

Back to football! The coaching staff of one football team with aspirations for national prestige was in the midst of its Sunday morning ritual—a strategy conference for the following Saturday afternoon game. The head coach asked the key question: "How can we move the ball on their defense?" A phone call then took him from the room, and during this time the staff discussed the problems posed by the opponent's defense. They unanimously agreed that the only way to beat that defense was to put great pressure on a certain defensive halfback by passing deep and out in his zone and combining this strategy with sweeps and pitch-outs at the same side.

The offensive backfield coach was the most outspoken in his support of that strategy. He particularly agreed that not only would it be a waste of time to attack the opponent up the middle, but that such an attack would probably result in a few maimed backs.

The head coach returned and announced, "Now as I see it, we must whip their middle. Defeat them up the gut and we'll own them." (While this was true, it was not likely to happen!)

The offensive backfield coach chimed in, "You're absolutely right, coach. Take it to 'em! Run over that Brutinski and we'll own 'em!"

The other coaches were not stunned; this happened every Sunday. No one bothered to mention that Brutinski was 15 feet tall, weighed 934 pounds, and ran the 40 in 3.4—at least that was the report of those backs who had tried to go through him previously and had survived to tell about it.

Oh yes, the final score: Brutinski, 35; Run-Over-Him U., 6. Some say Brutinski made All-American that afternoon.

That coaching staff had one good assistant—a new man who lasted for only one season because he gave contrary advice. This head coach only wanted to hear his own thoughts bounce back. He wanted yes-men, and administrators usually get what they want.

Therefore it must be concluded that wise counsels, from whomever they come, must necessarily be due to the prudence of the prince, and not the prudence of the prince to the good counsels received.

How Much Fortune Can Do in Human Affairs and How It May Be Opposed

IT IS NOT unknown to me how many have been and are of [the] opinion that worldly events are so governed by fortune and by God, that men cannot by their prudence change them, and that on the contrary there is no remedy whatever, and for this they may judge it to be useless to toil much about them, but let things be ruled by chance. This opinion has been more held in our day, from the great changes that have been seen, and are daily seen, beyond every human conjecture. When I think about them, at times I am partly inclined to share this opinion. Nevertheless, that our freewill may not be altogether extinguished,

111

I think it may be true that fortune is the ruler of half our actions, but that she allows the other half or thereabouts to be governed by us. I would compare her to an impetuous river that, when turbulent, inundates the plains, casts down trees and buildings, removes earth from this side and places it on the other; everyone flees before it, and everything yields to its fury without being able to oppose it; and yet though it is of such a kind, still when it is quiet, men can make provisions against it by dykes and banks, so that when it rises it will either go into a canal or its rush will not be so wild and dangerous. So it is with fortune, which shows her power where no measures have been taken to resist her, and directs her fury where she knows that no dykes or barriers have been made to hold her. And if you regard Italy, which has been the seat of these changes, and which has given the impulse to them, you will see her to be a country without dykes or banks of any kind. If she had been protected by proper measures, like Germany, Spain, and France, this inundation would not have caused the great changes that it has, or would not have happened at all.

This must suffice as regards opposition to fortune in general. But limiting myself more to particular cases, I would point out how one sees a certain prince today fortunate and tomorrow ruined, without seeing that he has changed in character or otherwise. I believe this arises in the first place from the causes that we have already discussed at length; that is to say, because the prince who bases himself entirely on fortune is ruined when fortune changes. I also believe that he is happy whose mode of procedure accords with the needs of the times, and similarly he is unfortunate whose mode of procedure is opposed to the times. For one sees that men in those things which lead them to the aim that each one has in view, namely, glory and riches, proceed in various ways; one with circumspection, another with impetuosity, one by violence, another by cunning, one with patience, another with the reverse; and each by these diverse ways may arrive at his aim. One sees also two cautious men, one of whom succeeds in his designs, and the other not, and in the same way two men succeed equally by different methods, one being cautious, the other impetuous, which arises only from the nature of the times, which does or does not conform to their method of procedure. From this it results, as I have said, that two men, acting differently, attain the same effect, and of two others acting in the same way, one attains his goal and not the other. On this depend also the changes in prosperity, for if it happens that time and circumstances are favourable to one who acts with caution and prudence, he will be successful, but if time and circumstances change, he will be ruined, because he does not change his mode of procedure. *No man is found so prudent as to be able to adapt himself to this, either because he cannot deviate from that to which his nature disposes him, or else because having always prospered by walking in one path, he cannot persuade himself that it is well to leave it; and therefore the cautious man, when it is time to act suddenly, does not know how to do so and is consequently ruined; for if one could change one's nature with time and circumstances, fortune would never change.*

The late Sewell Avery again serves as a case in point. His record for operating Montgomery Ward during the Great Depression was outstanding. He knew how to operate a firm in hard times, but the continued prosperity after World War II baffled him. He could only remain prepared for another depression. He could not become a manager of growth.

Bernie Bierman, a great single-wing coach at Min-
nesota, was unable to alter his teaching strategy to
successfully accommodate the T formation.

The current business scene is littered with the
career corpses of managers who knew how to be
successful in the wheeling-dealing stock markets of
the 1960s, where high price-earning ratios lubricated
their financial operations. When the money markets
tightened, these managers were lost. They did not
know what to do. Empires collapsed while men fled for
the West Indies and points south.

It is an extremely rare man who is able to alter his
ways to the dictates of fortune.

Pope Julius II acted impetuously in everything he did
and found the times and conditions so in conformity with
that mode of procedure, that he always obtained a good
result. Consider the first war that he made against Bologna
while Messer Giovanni Bentivogli was still living. The
Venetians were not pleased with it, neither was the King of
Spain, France was conferring with him over the enterprise, notwithstanding which, owing to his fierce and impetuous disposition, he engaged personally in the expedition. This move caused both Spain and the Venetians to
halt and hesitate, the latter through fear, the former
through the desire to recover the entire kingdom of Naples. On the other hand, he engaged with him the King of
France, because seeing him make this move and desiring
his friendship in order to put down the Venetians, that king
judged that he could not refuse him his troops without
manifest injury. Thus Julius by his impetuous move
achieved what no other pontiff with the utmost human
prudence would have succeeded in doing, because, if he
had waited till all arrangements had been made and every-

thing settled before leaving Rome, as any other pontiff would have done, it would never have succeeded. For the king of France would have found a thousand excuses, and the others would have inspired him with a thousand fears. I will omit his other actions, which were all of this kind and which all succeeded well, and the shortness of his life did not suffer him to experience the contrary, for had times followed in which it was necessary to act with caution, his ruin would have resulted, for he would never have deviated from these methods to which his nature disposed him.

I conclude then that fortune varying and men remaining fixed in their ways, they are successful so long as these ways conform to circumstances, but when they are opposed then they are unsuccessful.

Thus organizations are usually forced to seek the man whose ways conform to the needs of the times rather than the man who can change with the times, for the supply of the former is ample while the latter is a rarity.

I certainly think that it is better to be impetuous than cautious, for fortune is a woman, and it is necessary, if you wish to master her, to conquer her by force; and it can be seen that she lets herself be overcome by the bold rather than by those who proceed coldly.

A vote of confidence for the venturesome administrator. Those who don't take risks never give Dame Fortune a chance to work for them.

A good manager makes the right things happen —the things which seem to get bogged down under the direction of cautious men. The well-known tale of

the cautious Union generals during the Civil War is a
case in point. General Grant—for all his faults—made
things happen. He forced action to allow Fortune to
smile upon his efforts.

And therefore, like a woman, she is always a friend to the
young, because they are less cautious, fiercer, and master
her with greater audacity.

The Discourses
First Book

If an Able And Vigorous Prince Is Succeeded by a Feeble One, the Latter May for a Time Be Able to Maintain Himself; But If His Successor Be Also Weak, Then the Latter Will Not Be Able to Preserve His State

IN CAREFULLY examining the characters and conduct of Romulus, Numa, and Tullus, the first three kings of Rome, we see that she was favored by the greatest good fortune in having her first king courageous and warlike, the second peace-loving and religious, and the third equally courageous with Romulus, and preferring war to peace. For it was important for Rome that in the beginning there should arise a legislator capable of endowing her with civil institutions; but then it was essential that the succeeding kings should equal Romulus in virtue and valor, otherwise the city would have become effeminate and a prey to her neighbors. Whence we may note that a successor of less vigor and ability than the first king may yet be able to maintain a state established by the genius and courage of his predecessor and may enjoy the fruits of his labors. But if it should happen that his life be a long one, or that his successor should not have the same good qualities and courage as the first king, then the government will necessarily go to ruin. And so, on the contrary, if one king succeeds another of equally great abilities and courage, then it will often be seen that they achieve extraordinary greatness for their state, and that their fame will rise to the very heavens. David was beyond doubt a most extraordinary man in war, in learning, and in superior judgment; and such was his military ability that, having conquered and crushed his neighbors, he left a peaceful kingdom to his son Solomon, which he was able to maintain by the arts of peace and of war, and could thus happily enjoy the results of his father's virtue and valor. But he could not thus transmit it to his son, Rehoboam, who had neither the merits of his grandfather nor the good fortune of his father; and it was with difficulty, therefore, that he remained heir of the sixth part of the kingdom. The Sultan Bajazet of Turkey, although preferring peace to war, yet could enjoy the labors of his father Mahomet, who, having, like David, crushed his neighbors, left him a firmly established kingdom, which he could easily preserve with the arts of peace. But the empire would have gone to ruin if his son, Soliman the present Sultan, had resembled the father and not the grandfather; but it was seen that he even exceeded the glory of the grandfather.

I say then, that, according to these examples, the successor of a wise and vigorous prince, though himself feeble, may maintain a kingdom, even if it be not constituted like France, which is maintained by the force of its ancient institutions. . .

An able organization can stand a weak administrator, but only for so long. The affairs of men moved much slower in 1530 than they do in the 1970s. Today's business leader may make more decisions in one day than an Italian merchant prince made in a year. Since decisions are what get a weak administrator into trouble, a weak prince today would probably not last as long as he did in Machiavelli's day.

. . . and I call that prince feeble who is incapable of carrying on war. I conclude, then, that the genius and courage of Romulus were such that it left Numa competent to govern Rome for many years by the arts of peace. He was succeeded by Tullus, whose courage and warlike disposition exceeded even that of Romulus. After him came Ancus, who was gifted by nature to shine equally in peace and in war. At first he was disposed to follow the ways of peace, but he soon perceived that his neighbors regarded him as effeminate, and esteemed him but little; so that he concluded that, if he wished to maintain the Roman state, he must devote himself to war, and imitate Romulus, and not Numa Pompilius. Let all princes then who govern states take example from this, that he who follows the course of Numa may keep or lose his throne, according to chance and circumstances; but he who imitates the example of Romulus, and combines valor with prudence, will keep his throne anyhow, unless it be taken from him by some persistent and excessive force. And we may certainly assume that, if Rome had not chanced to have for her king a man who knew how by force of arms to restore her original reputation, she would not have been able, except with greatest difficulty, to gain a firm foothold and achieve the great things she did. And thus so long as she was governed by kings was she exposed to the danger of being ruined by a feeble or a wicked one.

One Should Never Risk One's Whole Fortune Unless Supported by One's Entire Forces, and Therefore the Mere Guarding of Passes Is Often Dangerous

IT WAS *never deemed wise to risk one's whole fortune with out employing at the same time one's whole forces, and which may be done in different ways.*

A prosperous CPA invested all of his modest fortune in a new enterprise formed to make and market a promising chemical specialty product. The venture floundered for want of management. The CPA saw what needed to be done, but was unable to spend the necessary time with the new venture because of the

demands of his own practice. He lost his money. He
had been willing to risk his fortune but not to commit his
total support to the investment.

Many new products introduced by large organizations fail because a company refuses to commit sufficient resources to insure the product's success. Long
ago, military tacticians learned the importance of keeping reserves ready to throw into the fray to turn the tide
of battle, and coaches have long recognized the importance of bench strength, but administrators seldom
include in their planning the need for reserves to support their efforts. Such reserves require budgeting.

One is the acting like Tullus and Metius, when they
committed the entire fortunes of their countries, and so
many brave men as both had in their armies, to the valor of
only three of their citizens, who constituted but a
minimum part of their respective forces. They did not
perceive that by so doing all the labors of their predeccos-
sors in organizing the republic so as to insure it a long and
free existence, and to make her citizens defenders of their
liberty, were as it were made nugatory, by putting it in the
power of so few to lose the whole. On the part of the
Romans, they could certainly not have done a more ill-
considered thing. The same fault is almost always committed by those who, upon the approach of an enemy, attempt
to hold the difficult approaches, and to guard the passes;
which course will almost always prove dangerous, unless
you can conveniently place all your forces there, in which
case that course may be adopted; but if the locality be so
rugged that you cannot keep and deploy all your forces
there, then it is dangerous. I am induced to think so by the
example of those who, when assailed by a powerful enemy,
their country being surrounded by mountains and rugged

places, never attempted to combat the enemy in the passes or mountains, but have always gone either to meet him in advance of these, or, when they did not wish to do that, have awaited his coming in easy and open places; the reason of which is the one I have above alleged. For you cannot employ a large force in guarding rugged and mountainous places; be it that you cannot obtain provisions there for any length of time, or that the defiles are so narrow as to admit of only a small number of men, so that it becomes impossible to sustain the shock of an enemy who comes in large force. Now for the enemy it is easy to come in full force, for his intention is to pass, and not to stop there; whilst on the contrary he who has to await the approach of the enemy cannot possibly keep so large a force there, for the reason that he will have to establish himself for a longer time in those confined and sterile places, not knowing when the enemy may come to make the attempt to pass. And once having lost the pass which you had hoped to hold, and upon which your people and army had confidently relied, they are generally seized with such terror that they are lost, without your having even been able to test their courage; and thus you lose your whole fortune from having risked only a portion of your forces.

It is well known what difficulties Hannibal encountered in passing the Alps that separate Lombardy from France, as well as the mountains the divide Lombardy from Tuscany; nevertheless, the Romans awaited him first on the Ticino, and afterwards in the plains of Arezzo; for they preferred rather to expose their army to being defeated in a place where they themselves had a chance of being the victors, than to move it to the mountains, to be destroyed there by the difficulties of the locality. And whoever reads history attentively will find that very few of the best commanders have attempted to hold such passes, for the very reasons which I have given, and because they cannot close them all the mountains being in that respect like the open country, in having not only well-known roads that are generally used, but also many others, which, if unknown to strangers, are yet familiar to the people of the country, by whose aid any invader may always be guided to any desired point. Of this we have a most notable and recent example in 1515, when Francis I, king of France, wanted to enter Italy for the purpose of recovering the state of Lombardy. Those who opposed him in this attempt, relied mainly upon their confident expectations that the Swiss would arrest his march in the mountain passes. But the event proved that their confidence was vain, for the king of France, leaving aside the two or three passes that were guarded by the Swiss, came by another route hitherto quite unknown, and was in Italy and upon them before they knew anything of it; so that their terror-stricken troops retreated to Milan, and the entire Milanese population yielded themselves to the French, having been disappointed in their hopes that the French would be kept out by difficulty of passing the Alps.

Well-Ordered Republics Establish Punishments and Rewards for Their Citizens, But Never Set Off One Against the Other

THE SERVICES of Horatius had been of the highest importance to Rome, for by his bravery he had conquered the Curatii; but the crime of killing his sister was atrocious, and the Romans were so outraged by this murder that he was put upon trial for his life, notwithstanding his recent great services to the state. Now, in looking at this matter superficially, it may seem like an instance of popular ingratitude; but a more careful examination, and reflection as to what the laws of a republic ought to be, will show that the people were to blame rather for the acquittal of Horatius than for having him tried. *And the reason for this is, that no*

127

well-ordered republic should ever cancel the crimes of its citizens by their merits; but having established rewards for good actions and penalties for evil ones, and having rewarded a citizen for good conduct who afterwards commits a wrong, he should be chastised for that without regard to his previous merits.

A most important management principle! Outstanding performance should never provide a cloak of immunity for the misdeeds of an individual.

When Kerry became sales manager for a housewares manufacturer, the sales force he inherited was unimpressive but there were a few rays of sunshine. One of them was Roy, a star performer. Kerry noted that Roy did not always follow directions and that his expenses were high, but he said nothing. Star salesmen are entitled to such privileges, or so the thinking goes in some circles.

The trouble was that Roy did not perceive his limits. His expense accounts kept growing and his work degenerated. Finally Kerry had a talk with Roy about the problem, but to no avail. So Kerry limited Roy's expenses, specifically his telephone expenses. Told not to go over $100 per month, Roy defied the order by turning in a $220 telephone bill the following month, as if to test Kerry's resolution. Roy did not know his man. He was fired and his excess expenses were deducted from his severance pay—an unfortunate incident that might have been avoided had Roy's misdeeds been disciplined from the first.

To excuse one crime invites another. When finally apprehended, the culprit feels the rules are not being uniformly applied: "Suddenly they change the rules on me!"

And a state that properly observes this principle will long enjoy its liberty; but if otherwise, it will speedily come to ruin. For if a citizen who has rendered some eminent service to the state should add to the reputation and influence which he has thereby acquired the confident audacity of being able to commit any wrong without fear of punishment, he will in a little while become so insolent and overbearing as to put an end to all power of the law. But to preserve a wholesome fear of punishment for evil deeds, it is necessary not to omit rewarding good ones; as has been seen was done by Rome. And although a republic may be poor and able to give but little, yet she should not abstain from giving that little; for even the smallest reward for a good action—no matter how important the service to the state—will always be esteemed by the recipient as most honorable. The story of Horatius Cocles and of Mutius Scaevola is well known; how the one, single-handed, kept back the enemy to give time for the destruction of a bridge, and how the other burned his hand off for having erred in his attempt to take the life of Porsenna, king of the Tuscans. As a reward for their eminent services the city of Rome gave to each of them two acres of land. The story of Manlius Capitolinus is equally well known; having saved the Capitol from the Gauls who were besieging it, he received from each of those who had been shut up in it with him a small measure of flour, which (according to the current prices of things in those days in Rome) was a reward of considerable value and importance. But when Manlius afterwards, inspired by envy or his evil nature, attempted to stir up a rebellion, and sought to gain the people over to himself, he was, regardless of his former services, precipitated from that very Capitol which it had been his previous glory to have saved.

Perhaps President Truman read this passage during his deliberations over what to do with General MacArthur during the Korean conflict.

Whoever Wishes to Reform an Existing Government in a Free State Should at Least Preserve the Semblance of the Old Forms

HE WHO desires or attempts to reform the government of a state, and wishes to have it accepted and capable of maintaining itself to the satisfaction of everybody, must at least retain the semblance of the old forms; so that it may seem to the people that there has been no change in the institutions, even though in fact they are entirely different from the old ones. For the great majority of mankind are satisfied with appearances, as though they were realities, and are often even more influenced by the things that seem than by those that are. The Romans understood this well, and for that reason, when they first recovered their liberty, and had created two Consuls in place of a king, they would not allow these more than twelve lictors, so as not to exceed the number that had served the king. Besides this, the Romans were accustomed to an annual sacrifice that could only be performed by the king in person; and as they did not wish that the people, in consequence of the absence of the king, should have occasion to regret the loss of any of their old customs, they created a special chief for that ceremony, whom they called the king of the sacrifice, and placed him under their high priest; so that the people enjoyed these annual sacrificial ceremonies, and had no pretext, from the want of them, for desiring the restoration of the kings. *And this rule should be observed by all who wish to abolish an existing system of government in any state, and introduce a new and more liberal one. For as all novelties excite the minds of men, it is important to retain in such innovations as much as possible the previously existing forms.*

> An amplification of the earlier warning about the dangers of instituting a new order of things.
> Many excellent recommendations for the reform of the evils existent in higher education have been made, but they generally fail to gain much of a hearing when they challenge the sacred credit-hour system, the traditional role of the professor and his way of life, or the powers of the departments and schools. Most realistic reforms have to conform to the existing order of academic affairs.

And if the number, authority, and duration of the term of service of the magistrates be changed, the titles at least ought to be preserved. This, as I have said, should be observed by whoever desires to convert an absolute government either into a republic or a monarchy; but, on the contrary, he who wishes to establish an absolute power, such as ancient writers called a tyranny, must change everything, as we shall show in the following chapter.

A New Prince in a City or Province Conquered by Him Should Organize Everything Anew

WHOEVER *becomes prince* of a city or state, especially if the foundation of his power is feeble, and does not wish to establish there either a monarchy or a republic, *will find the best means for holding that principality to organize the government entirely anew* . . .

New coaches generally recognize the need for bringing a completely new staff with them. Rare is the assistant coach who can successfully transfer his allegiance to a new man. Moreover, the new coach is never sure what role the assistant played in the previous coach's failure. Many professional administrators bring an entire staff or team with them.

A new college president retained his unfortunate predecessor's staff and all of his vice presidents. The previous president had been fired for various failures, which, in fact, had largely been due to his subordinates. His mistake had been in his choice of a team; his staff had been responsible for the difficulties for which he was blamed. True to form, these incompetents nailed their second president with the same lack of performance. The next president cleaned house and still holds the thankless job. You can be safe in assuming that if a man fails in a job, his subordinates are partly to blame. Good subordinates protect their bosses.

Did you catch old Nick in his apparent inconsistency? In Chapter Six of *The Prince*, he came on strong about the dangers awaiting administrators who try "to initiate a new order of things." Yet now he urges organizing one's government anew. How come? It would seem that here he is talking about changing bodies only—not changing the system, the order of things. But how realistic is it to change bodies and not reap a change in order? Not very. So there is a problem here.

I suspect it is more important to bring in your own people than it is to worry about the existing system. And I also suspect that systems or orders can be altered somewhat as circumstances indicate. Many systems are screaming for change; perhaps that's why you were brought in.

The key to changing a system may be to devise ways to make changes that do not threaten the security of those people you want to keep. The new system must provide your key people with the benefits they seek.

. . . (he being himself a new prince there); that is, he should appoint new governors with new titles, new powers, and new men, and he should make the poor rich, as David did when he became king, "who heaped riches upon the needy, and dismissed the wealthy empty-handed."

Besides this, he should destroy the old cities and build new ones, and transfer the inhabitants from one place to another; in short, he should leave nothing unchanged in that province, so that there should be neither rank, nor grade, nor honor, nor wealth, that should not be recognized as coming from him. He should take Philip of Macedon, father of Alexander, for his model, who by proceeding in that manner became, from a petty king, master of all Greece. And his historian tells us that he transferred the inhabitants from one province to another, as shepherds move their flocks from place to place. Doubtless these means are cruel and destructive of all civilized life, and neither Christian nor even human, and should be avoided by everyone. In fact, the life of a private citizen would be preferable to that of a king at the expense of the ruin of so many human beings. Nevertheless, whoever is unwilling to adopt the first and humane course must, if he wishes to maintain his power, follow the latter evil course. But men generally decide upon a middle course, which is most hazardous; for they know neither how to be entirely good or entirely bad.

When an Evil Has Sprung Up Within a State, or Come Upon It from Without, It Is Safer to Temporize with It Rather Than to Attack It Violently

As THE Roman republic grew in reputation, power, and dominion, the neighboring tribes, who at first had not thought of how great a danger this new republic might prove to them, began (too late, however) to see their error; and wishing to remedy their first neglect, they united full forty tribes in a league against Rome. Hereupon the Romans resorted, amongst other measures which they were accustomed to employ in urgent dangers, to the creation of a dictator, that is to say, they gave the power to one man, who, without consulting anyone else, could determine upon any course, and could have it carried into effect without any appeal. This measure, which on former occasions had proved most useful in overcoming imminent perils, was equally serviceable to them in all the critical events that occurred during the growth and development of the power of the republic. Upon this subject we must remark, first, that when any evil arises within a republic or threatens it from without, that is to say, from an intrinsic or extrinsic cause, and has become so great as to fill everyone with apprehension, the more certain remedy by far is to temporize with it, rather than to attempt to extirpate it; *for almost invariably he who attempts to crush it will rather increase its force, and will accelerate the harm apprehended from it.*

This should surprise many managers, who might have guessed that Machiavelli would urge quick reaction to evil. Some authorities would vehemently disagree with Niccolò's point, contending that the quicker you nail evil, the better off you will be. The resolution of this argument lies in the precise nature of the evil. Some evils can be temporized, others cannot. If a problem arises in quality control, quick action is required. If sales fall off in a key territory, most sales managers will act immediately. If somebody is tapping the till, he won't stop it without some assistance. Many business problems (evils) require quick reactions. The usual difficulty is in perceiving the problem too late to take action to minimize the damage.

Machiavelli was probably speaking of situations in which one is apt to act unwisely and in haste due to a lack of facts, the possession of untruths or an emotional reaction. Upon first appraisal of an evil, it is unlikely that the administrator will have a sufficiently good grasp of the situation to enable him to react to it. Time can clarify the matter.

And such evils arise more frequently in a republic from intrinsic than extrinsic causes, as it often occurs that a citizen is allowed to acquire more authority than is proper; or that changes are permitted in a law which is the very nerve and life of liberty; and then they let this evil go so far that it becomes more hazardous to correct it than to allow it to run on. *And it is the more difficult to recognize these evils at their origin, as it seems natural to men always to favor the beginning of things; and these favors are more readily accorded to such acts as seem to have some merit in them and are done by young men.*

And here we have the root of a great many bad business situations. Most people find it difficult to perceive the evil inherent in a new program during its early stages, and those who do see the flaws of a new program may be silenced by any one of a number of reasons: They don't care; they're afraid of reprisals; they lack confidence or power. Or perhaps their cries of protest are overridden by those who worship the new, regardless of its merit. Some people in particular seem to feel strongly that they must find some way to discredit the work of others in order to rise more rapidly in the order. And what better way than to supplant the work of others—and their old programs—with new ventures?

For if in a republic a noble youth is seen to rise, who is possessed of some extraordinary merits, the eyes of all citizens quickly turn to him, and all hasten to show him honor, regardless of consequences; so that, if he is in any way ambitious, the gifts of nature and the favor of his fellow-citizens will soon raise him to such a height that, when the citizens become sensible of the error they have committed, they have no longer the requisite means for checking him, and their efforts to employ such as they have will only accelerate his advance to power.

The names of some recent political heroes might fit into this scene. The problem is that people want heroes—want them so badly that they will seize at whatever heroic straws are available, carefully ignoring dissonant factors or rationalizing them away to retain their image of their hero. Hero images can weather unbelievable storms. The hero is believed; his tormentors are chastised.

At any time on the American business scene, the trade press can be heard trumpeting the career of some "boy wonder." Seldom is there a shortage of wonder boys, yet history has dealt harshly with most of these men. Experience usually discloses that their reputed talents are more frequently the creation of an ingenious public-relations man than real skills. Nevertheless, the boy wonder is given a great deal of latitude until reality finally closes in on his career —although sometimes it never does. While my instincts scream to name names here, my lawyer assures me it would be financial folly to do so.

Many instances of this might be cited, but I will confine myself to one which occurred in our own city of Florence. Cosimo de' Medici, to whom the house of Medici owes the beginning of its greatness, obtained such reputation and authority through his own sagacity and the ignorance of his fellow-citizens, that he became a cause of apprehension to the government and that the other citizens judged it hazardous to offend him but more dangerous still to allow him to go on. At that time there lived in Florence Niccolò Uzzano, reputed a man of consummate ability in matters of state, who, having committed the first error of not foreseeing the danger that might result from the great influence of Cosimo, would never permit the Florentines, so long as he lived, to commit the second error of trying to destroy Cosimo, judging that any such attempt would lead to the ruin of the state, as in fact proved to be the case after his death. For the citizens, regardless of the counsels of Uzzano, combined against Cosimo and drove him from Florence. The consequence was that the partisans of Cosimo, to resent this insult, shortly afterwards recalled him and made him prince of the republic, which position he never would have attained but for the previous hostility manifested towards him. The same thing happened in Rome with regard to Caesar, who by his courage and merits at first won the favor of Pompey and of other prominent citizens, but which favor was shortly after converted into fear; to which Cicero testifies, saying "that Pompey had begun too late to fear Caesar." This fear caused them to think of measures of safety, which however only accelerated the ruin of the republic.

I say, then, that inasmuch as it is difficult to know these evils at their first origin, owing to an illusion which all new things are apt to produce, the wiser course is to temporize with such evils when they are recognized, instead of violently attacking them; for by temporizing with them they will either die out of themselves, or at least their worst results will be long deferred.

It is difficult to spot evil early, but this is a talent good administrators try to develop to some extent: Anticipate trouble and avoid it. The problem seems to be that it is easier to ignore evil in the hope either that it will not develop or that it will go away.

Then, too, an administrator is apt to be shielded from "evil" by his subordinates, who may fear that the evil will reflect unfavorably upon their own performances. Subordinates are ever watchful, hoping to deal with the "evil" before it is noticed by the boss. Upward communication channels are usually well blockaded to all but the perceptive administrator who has managed to evade the barriers.

Moreover, there is the problem of interpreting the evil and deciding what direction it is likely to take. Most of the world's political leaders failed miserably in their interpretation of the Nazi movement in Germany during the early 1930s and were not prepared for the direction it took.

Then there are the problems of discerning when to act, what to do, and how much of a remedy the evil requires. Generalizations cannot be made; it comes down to a matter of executive judgment. Machiavelli merely urges that you go easy, that you don't rush in swinging wildly, until you have the whole picture well in mind.

Finally, the innate laziness of man must be cited. It is always easier to do nothing than to do something, so the mind makes up fairy tales to justify its inaction.

And princes or magistrates who wish to destroy such evils must watch all points, and must be careful in attacking them not to increase instead of diminish them, for they must not believe that a fire can be extinguished by blowing upon it. *They should carefully examine the extent and force of the evil, and if they think themselves sufficiently strong to combat it, then they should attack it regardless of conse-*

quences; otherwise they should let it be, and in no wise attempt it.

Don't act unless you have the power to get the job done. But judging your own power is not an easy task. Overestimating it can produce disastrous results.

For it will always happen as I have said above, and as it did happen to the neighboring tribes of Rome, who found that it would have been more advantageous, after Rome had grown so much in power, to placate and keep her within her limits by peaceful means, than by warlike measures to make her think of new institutions and new defences. For their league had no other effect than to unite the people of Rome more closely, and to make them more ready for war, and to cause them to adopt new institutions that enabled them in a brief time to increase their power. One of these was the creation of a Dictator, by which new institution they not only overcame the most imminent dangers, but obviated also an infinity of troubles in which they would otherwise have been involved.

What Troubles Resulted in Rome from the Enactment of the Agrarian Law, and How Very Wrong It Is to Make Laws That Are Retrospective and Contrary to Old Established Customs

IT WAS a saying of ancient writers, that men afflict themselves in evil and become weary of the good, and that both these dispositions produce the same effects. *For when men are no longer obliged to fight from necessity, they fight from ambition, which passion is so powerful in the hearts of men that it never leaves them, no matter to what height they may rise. The reason of this is that nature has created men so that they desire everything, but are unable to attain it; desire being thus always greater than the faculty of acquiring, discontent with what they have and dissatisfaction with themselves result from it.*

It is amazing to witness successful people. Whatever they have, it is never enough. At a dinner party, a young professor complained to a multimillionaire that he was not making "enough." She coldly turned to him and said, "Young man, it is never enough!" That summarizes it rather well.

No matter how well you pay your subordinates, you may rest assured that they will want more and will become discontented if they don't get it. Many have abandoned sound situations for careers that promise more, only to discover that not all promises are kept. Greed seems to blind us to the realities of the situation as we manipulate our minds to rationalize that we are worth more than we are being paid.

This causes the changes in their fortunes; for as some men desire to have more, whilst others fear to lose what they have, enmities and war are the consquences; and this brings about the ruin of one province and the elevation of another.

The Same Accidents Often Happen to Different Peoples

WHOEVER considers the past and the present will readily observe that all cities and all peoples are and ever have been animated by the same desires and the same passions; so that it is easy, by diligent study of the past, to foresee what is likely to happen in the future in any republic, and to apply those remedies that were used by the ancients, or, not finding any that were employed by them, to devise new ones from the similarity of the events. But as such considerations are neglected or not understood by most of those who read, or, if understood by these, are unknown by those who govern, *it follows that the same troubles generally recur in all republics.*

> And the same goes for businesses! Thus the value of experience is explained. The manager who has been around for some time is likely to have been through a given trouble before; hence, he will be in a better position to handle it than an inexperienced person will be.

It Is a Bad Example Not to Observe the Laws, Especially on the Part of Those Who Have Made Them; and It Is Dangerous for Those Who Govern Cities to Harass the People with Constant Wrongs

THE agreement between the Senate and the people having been carried into effect, and Rome restored to her ancient form of government, Virginius cited Appius before the people to defend his cause. He appeared accompanied by many nobles. Virginius insisted upon his being imprisoned, whereupon Appius loudly demanded to appeal to the people. Virginius maintained that he was unworthy of the privilege of that appeal, which he had himself destroyed, and not entitled to have for his defenders the very people whom he had offended. Appius replied that the people had no right to violate that appeal which they themselves had instituted with so much jealousy. But he was nevertheless incarcerated, and before the day of judgment came he committed suicide. And although the crimes of Appius merited the highest degree of punishment, yet it was inconsistent with a proper regard for liberty to violate the law, and especially one so recently made. *For I think that there can be no worse example in a republic than to make a law and not to observe it; the more so when it is disregarded by the very parties who made it.*

Nor will an able administrator make any rules that he does not intend to keep himself. Ted Williams once made a rule that anyone late for a game would be fined $150. And guess what! Yes—and he kicked in the $150, with no urging or whimpering. Now there's a manager! Not only are double standards deeply resented but they also ultimately result in contempt for the rule in question and violation of it whenever possible.

Upon assumption of his duties, a new chief administrator for an educational unit made it plain to his faculty that they were not only to convene all classes but that they were also to keep office hours and attend all meetings. Not an unreasonable request—although a few unbridled souls were restless, while the cynics smiled unperturbed. Soon the administrator's colors were flying for all to see. He was seldom in his office: "out-of-town consulting." He missed meetings. His favorites among the faculty were the worst offenders. Yet each year he would repeat his rules to the new faculty members, while some of the older members snickered and others stood sad and silent. No one respected him; some left for other pastures.

Think about the rules you are about to lay down. Are you really prepared to abide by them, or are you laying down a smoke screen?

In the year 1494 Florence had reformed its government with the aid of Brother Girolamo Savonarola (whose writings exhibit so much learning, prudence, and courage); and amongst other provisions for the security of the citizens a law had been made which permitted an appeal to the people from the decisions which the Council of Eight and the Signoria might render in cases affecting the state, which had involved great discussions and difficulties in its passage. It happened that shortly after its confirmation five citizens were condemned to death by the Signoria on account of crimes against the state; and when these men wished to appeal to the people, they were not allowed to do so, in manifest disregard of the law. This occurrence did more than anything else to diminish the influence of Savonarola; for if the appeal was useful, then the law should have been observed, and if it was not useful, then it should never have been made. And this circumstance was the more remarked, as Brother Girolamo in his many subsequent preachings never condemned those who had broken the law, and rather excused the act in the manner of one unwilling to condemn what suited his purposes, yet unable to excuse it wholly. Having thus manifested his ambitious and partial spirit, it cost him his reputation and much trouble.

A government also does great wrong constantly to excite the resentment of its subjects by fresh injuries to this or that individual amongst them.

So simple a principle that one wonders. Perhaps the offending administrator fails to perceive the reign of terror he has instilled. It happens! Such administrators seldom last long, but the damage they can do in a short time is frightening.

One new basketball coach for a leading university so outraged his players with daily insults and injuries that he had only eight men—all bench-warming material—to start the season. One game was finished with three men on the floor. He did not last long at the university, and he is no longer a coach.

This principle helps to explain some of the difficulties governments encounter in combating guerrilla and revolutionary forces over a long period of time. A government, in restraining such efforts, is forced to commit a certain number of injuries, some of which are bound to be unjust. Then, if the fight lasts long enough, the government may become the enemy as the people become incensed over the continued injustices. This principle eventually worked against some campus rioters: Their fellow students finally got tired of the terror and began turning on their own.

This was the case after the Decemvirate, for all the Ten and many other citizens were at different times accused and condemned, so as to create the greatest alarm amongst the nobles, for it seemed as though these condemnations would never cease until the entire nobility should have been destroyed. All this would have produced the worst effects if the Tribune Marcus Duellius had not prevented it by issuing an edict that for the period of one year no one should be allowed to cite or accuse a Roman citizen, and this reassured the whole nobility. These examples show how dangerous it is for a republic or a prince to keep the minds of their subjects in a state of apprehension by pains and penalties constantly suspended over their heads. And certainly no more pernicious course could be pursued; for men who are kept in doubt and uncertainty as to their lives will resort to every kind of measure to secure themselves against danger, and will necessarily become more audacious and inclined to violent changes. It is important, therefore, either never to attack any one, or to inflict punishment by a single act of rigor, and afterwards to reassure the public mind by such acts as will restore calmness and confidence.

A Republic or a Prince Must Feign to Do of Their Own Liberality That to Which Necessity Compels Them

PRUDENT *men make the best of circumstances in their actions, and, although constrained by necessity to a certain course, make it appear as if done from their own liberality.*

When an administrator is forced against his wishes to do something that will be regarded by others as good, then he should at least make it appear as if he is taking the action because of his own goodness. A merchant who knew that the minimum wage would soon go up to

$1.65 an hour "voluntarily" increased the wages of his clerks to that level a short time prior to the deadline.

But Machiavelli did not cover the opposite situation—making certain that you are not given credit for doing something unpopular that you are being forced to do. There are many common situations in which an administrator may shift the blame for some unpopular decision onto someone else. The use of hatchet men to fire employees is a prime example of this tactic.

This discretion was wisely used by the Roman Senate when they resolved to pay the soldiery out of the public treasury, who before had been obliged to maintain themselves. But as the Senate perceived that war could not be carried on for a length of time in this manner, as they could neither lay siege to places nor move armies to a distance, and judging it necessary to be able to do both, they resolved to pay them from the public funds; yet they did it in such a manner as to gain credit for that to which necessity compelled them; and this favor was so acceptable to the populace that Rome was wild with joy, thinking it a great benefit, which they had never expected and would not have sought themselves. And although the Tribunes endeavored to expose this delusion, showing that it made the burden of the people heavier instead of easier, still they could not prevent its acceptance by the people. This burden was further increased by the manner in which the Senate levied the taxes, imposing the heaviest and largest upon the nobility, and requiring them to pay first of all.

How by the Delusions of Seeming Good the People Are Often Misled to Desire Their Own Ruin; and How They Are Frequently Influenced by Great Hopes and Brave Promises

IF WE consider now what is easy and what [is] difficult to persuade a people to, we may make this distinction: Either what you wish to persuade them to represents at first sight gain or loss, or it seems brave or cowardly. *And if you propose to them anything that upon its face seems profitable and courageous, though there be really a loss concealed under it which may involve the ruin of the republic, the multitude will ever be most easily persuaded to it.*

People base decisions on potential profits, not on realities. The oil-drilling funds in recent years are grim

159

testimony to this truth. The salesmen chant "tax shelter" to some rich economic illiterates and they cough up millions of dollars in the hope of making a cheap tax killing. Most of them have not made one. The real economics of a situation are ignored for the promise of riches. Yell "get rich quick," and some greedy fools will heed the call.

There are two forces at work here. First, greed blinds men to the realities of a situation. We so strongly desire riches—so desperately seek all the good things we think money will bestow upon us—that our minds choose to either ignore or severely discount all evidence that threatens our greedy endeavors. We seem to have filters on our senses that only admit favorable facts.

Second, our culture has taught us to honor those people who display bold, imaginative action. The thought of Mr. Tucker competing with General Motors caught the admiration of many people, despite the asininity of the whole affair. We like to think that David will whip Goliath, but wise men bet Goliath across the board every time.

But if the measure proposed seems doubtful and likely to cause loss, then it will be difficult to persuade the people to it, even though the benefit and welfare of the republic were concealed under it.

The Discourses
Second Book

Introduction

MEN EVER praise the olden time, and find fault with the present, though often without reason. They are such partisans of the past that they extol not only the times which they know only by the accounts left of them by historians, but, having grown old, they also laud all they remember to have seen in their youth. Their opinion is generally erroneous in that respect, and I think the reasons which cause this illusion are various. *The first I believe to be the fact that we never know the whole truth about the past, and very frequently writers conceal such events as would reflect disgrace upon their century, whilst they magnify and amplify those that lend lustre to it.*

How true! You cannot even believe a first-hand account, for a participant may twist the truth or tell an
outright lie to place himself in the best possible light.

History is written by the victors; the vanquished tell a
different tale, but we seldom get to hear it.

Even stories appearing in periodicals can be misleading: Some are the creations of men who are trying
to sell their particular bill of goods, while others are a
result of inept reporting. Whatever, care must be taken
in reading what is being passed off as history.

One drug company, recounting its test-market failure of a new product in a leading sales magazine,
blamed the intrinsic nature of the item. It had failed to
sell in adequate volume in the Denver test market after
a "saturation" advertising promotion campaign in that
area. Well, I lived in Denver at the time of this alleged
test marketing, and there was no evidence of such a
campaign or a product in the city then. You figure it out!

The majority of authors obey the fortune of conquerors
to that degree that, by way of rendering their victories
more glorious, they exaggerate not only the valiant deeds
of the victor, but also of the vanquished; so that future
generations of the countries of both will have cause to
wonder at those men and times, and are obliged to praise
and admire them to the utmost.

History feeds on action and glorifies those who partake
in it, regardless of the outcome in most cases. Custer
was history's hero, although considered judgment can
only conclude he was the consummate fool. Truman
was lauded for Korea—a war on the Asian mainland
that military strategists have warned against for centuries. Roosevelt, Churchill, and MacArthur were all

lauded for their actions. Eisenhower has been criti-
cized by many people for heading a "do-nothing" administration. All we had was peace and prosperity, and
history can't tolerate such nonsense. It feeds on conflicts. So let it be known by all that history is an out-
landish fraud devoid of real content—of what actually
happened to the people. Perhaps the most significant
socioeconomic catastrophe in recent times was the
Great Depression of the 1930s, yet most basic history
books give it but a chapter. The lessons it taught have
been lost to the present generation because history
failed to preserve them.

Another reason is that men's hatreds generally spring
from fear or envy. Now, these two powerful reasons of
hatred do not exist for us with regard to the past, which can
no longer inspire either apprehension or envy. But it is
very different with the affairs of the present, in which we
ourselves are either actors or spectators, and of which we
have a complete knowledge, nothing being concealed from
us; and knowing the good together with many other things
that are displeasing to us, we are forced to conclude that
the present is inferior to the past, though in reality it may
be much more worthy of glory and fame. I do not speak of
matters pertaining to the arts, which shine by their intrinsic merits, which time can neither add to nor diminish; but
I speak of such things as pertain to the actions and manners
of men, of which we do not possess such manifest evidence.

I repeat, then, that this practise of praising and decrying
is very general, though it cannot be said that it is always
erroneous; for sometimes our judgment is of neccessity
correct, human affairs being in a state of perpetual movement, always either ascending or declining. We see, for
instance, a city or country with a government well or-

ganized by some man of superior ability; for a time it progresses and attains a great prosperity through the talents of its lawgiver. Now, if anyone living at such a period should praise the past more than the time in which he lives, he would certainly be deceiving himself; and this error will be found due to the reasons above indicated. But should he live in that city or country at the period after it shall have passed the zenith of its glory and in the time of its decline, then he would not be wrong in praising the past.

Money Is Not the Sinews of War, Although It Is Generally So Considered

EVERYONE may begin a war at his pleasure, but cannot so finish it. A prince, therefore, before engaging in any enterprise should well measure his strength, and govern himself accordingly; and he must be very careful not to deceive himself in the estimate of his strength, *which he will assuredly do if he measures it by his money, or by the situation of his country, or the good disposition of his people, unless he has at the same time an armed force of his own.*

What better proof than Vietnam? When will we learn the limitations of money? Corporate leadership is

scarcely better. With its great wealth, General Electric
thought that it could develop a position in the computer
industry. Year after year, G.E. poured millions of dollars into the fiasco until it finally threw in the towel and
sold the operation to Honeywell. It will be interesting to
see if Honeywell will be any more successful.

For although the above things will increase his strength,
yet they will not give it to him, and of themselves are
nothing, and will be of no use without a devoted army.
Neither abundance of money nor natural strength of the
country will suffice, nor will the loyalty and good will of his
subjects endure, for these cannot remain faithful to a
prince who is incapable of defending them. Neither mountains nor lakes nor inaccessible places will present any
difficulties to an enemy where there is a lack of brave
defenders. *And money alone, so far from being a means of
defence, will only render a prince the more liable to being
plundered. There cannot, therefore, be a more erroneous
opinion than that money is the sinews of war.*

When the history of mergers is written, the stockholders of several rich companies will be looking for
some administrators with a bucket of tar, a load of
feathers, and some rough rails. The United Shoe experience is a case in point. That venerable, rich Bosto-
nian empire was brought to the verge of bankruptcy by
a management that believed, in its administrative arrogance, that it could diversify successfully simply by
buying what appeared to be sound, growing enterprises. Money is of no help in choosing property. It only
serves to numb the sense of value. A wealthy man
tends to pay too much for what he buys. A poorer man
is a bit more aggressive in his bargaining.
    Many a manager has been deluded into thinking that
money will buy a "fighting army." If money could buy

performance, the Red Sox would be perennial world's champions, for Tom Yawkey has been most generous with his "soldiers."

I maintain, then, contrary to the general opinion, that the sinews of war are not gold, but good soldiers; *for gold alone will not procure good soldiers, but good soldiers will always procure gold.*

And there we have it! Your key to success lies with your employees. You can't win with poor players.

Had the Romans attempted to make their wars with gold instead of with iron, all the treasure of the world would not have sufficed them, considering the great enterprises they were engaged in, and the difficulties they had to encounter. But by making their wars with iron, they never suffered for the want of gold; for it was brought to them, even into their camp, by those who feared them. And if want of money forced the king of Sparta to try the fortune of battle, it was no more than what often happened from other causes; for we have seen that armies short of provisions, and having to starve or hazard a battle, will always prefer the latter as the more honorable course, and where fortune may yet in some way favor them. It has also often happened that a general, seeing that his opposing enemy is about to receive reinforcements, has preferred to run the risk of a battle at once, rather than wait until his enemy is reinforced and fight him then under greater disadvantage. We have seen also in the case of Asdrubal, when he was attacked upon the river Metaurus by Claudius Nero, together with another Roman Consul, that a general who has to choose between battle or flight will always prefer to fight, as then even in the most doubtful case, there is still a chance of victory, whilst in flight his loss is certain anyhow.

There are, then, an infinity of reasons that may induce a general to give battle against his will, and the want of money may in some instances be one of them; but that is no reason why money should be deemed the sinews of war, which more than anything else will influence him to that course. I repeat it again, then, that it is not gold, but good soldiers, that insure success in war. Certainly money is a necessity, but a secondary one, which good soldiers will overcome; for it is as impossible that good soldiers should not be able to procure gold, as it is impossible for gold to procure good soldiers. History proves in a thousand cases what I maintain, notwithstanding that Pericles counselled the Athenians to make war with the entire Peloponnesus, demonstrating to them that by perseverance and the power of money they would be successful. And although it is true that the Athenians obtained some successes in that war, yet they succumbed in the end; and good counsels and the good soldiers of Sparta prevailed over the perseverance and money of the Athenians. But the testimony of Titus Livius upon this question is more direct than any other, where, in discussing whether Alexander the Great, had he come into Italy, would have vanquished the Romans, he points out that there are three things preeminently necessary to success in war—plenty of good troops, sagacious commanders, and good fortune; and in examining afterwards whether the Romans or Alexander excelled most in these three points, he draws his conclusion without ever mentioning the subject of money. The Campanians, when requested by the Sidicians to take up arms in their behalf against the Samnites, may have measured their strength by their money, and not by their soldiers; for having resolved to grant the required assistance, they were constrained after two defeats to become tributary to the Romans to save themselves.

Cunning and Deceit Will Serve a Man Better Than Force to Rise from a Base Condition to Great Fortune

I BELIEVE *it to be most true that it seldom happens that men rise from low condition to high rank without employing either force or fraud . . .*

Naturally, critics will seize upon this passage as proof of Machiavelli's lack of scruples, but in cold review, he is merely relating what he believes to be true and is not recommending behavior. Of course, there is the problem of definition: What does he mean by "force"; what constitutes "fraud"? But it is unlikely that we can resolve this problem here, so let's rely on the conven-

171

tional usages of these terms. Fraud means deception and force simply means force. Anyone who considers the use of force to attain power archaic should bear in mind the fame gained by professional athletes, whose main weapon is some sort of force. And how about the Mafia? The labor unions? Minority political groups? College students? Force has not been forgotten by the Now generation.

But fraud is a bit more pleasant to write about, and it is so abundant that examples are available at every turn.

A promising, young, assistant coach obtained the head coaching job at a major football power by stampeding the board of regents into making him an offer before it could interview another man who, on paper, was the better choice. The young man had told them, "I have an offer from Touchdown U. to which I must reply this afternoon at five. I plan to accept it unless you make me an offer. I would prefer to win for you."

The regents knew that Touchdown U. had made him an offer—it had been in the papers—so they believed the rest of his story. They loved him, so he had the job on the spot. He told me later that he had had no intention of going to Touchdown U—that it was merely bush league and he was Big Time Charlie. Is that cunning or simply hard bargaining?

In all candor, after carefully reviewing the careers of all the leaders with whom I have been associated, without exception there were *numerous* incidents in each career from which one might conclude that deception was used to gain position. In fact, in a great many instances, the administrator who does not practice some deception would not only be considered simple, but his career would be at an end. Suppose you are firing a man because he is hopelessly incompetent; it may be best to protect his ego by telling him a different story. In bargaining, there can be many reasons to deceive the other party.

. . . unless that rank should be attained either by gift or inheritance. Nor do I believe that *force* alone will ever be found to suffice, whilst it will often be the case that *cunning* alone serves the purpose; as is clearly seen by whoever reads the life of Philip of Macedon, or that of Agathocles the Sicilian, and many others, who from the lowest or most moderate condition have achieved thrones and great empires. Xenophon shows in his Life of Cyrus the necessity of deception to success: the first expedition of Cyrus against the king of Armenia is replete with fraud, and it was deceit alone, and not force, that enabled him to seize that kingdom. And Xenophon draws no other conclusion from it than that a prince who wishes to achieve great things must learn to deceive. Cyrus also practised a variety of deceptions upon Cyaxares, king of the Medes, his maternal uncle; and Xenophon shows that without these frauds Cyrus would never have achieved the greatness which he did attain. Nor do I believe that there was ever a man who from obscure condition arrived at great power by merely employing open force; but there are many who have succeeded by fraud alone, as, for instance, Giovanni Galeazzo Visconti in taking the state and sovereignty of Lombardy from his uncle, Messer Bernabo. And that which princes are obliged to do in the beginning of their rise, republics are equally obliged to practise until they have become powerful enough so that force alone suffices them. And as Rome employed every means, by chance or choice, to promote her aggrandizement, so she also did not hesitate to employ fraud; nor could she have practised a greater fraud than by taking the course we have explained above of making other peoples her allies and associates, and under that title making them slaves, as she did with the Latins and neighboring nations. For first she availed of their arms to subdue their mutual neighbors, and thus to increase her state and reputation; and after having subdued these, her

power increased to that degree that she could subjugate
each people separately in turn. The Latins never became
aware that they were wholly slaves until they had witnes-
sed two defeats of the Samnites, and saw them obliged to
accept the terms of peace dictated to them. As this victory
greatly increased the reputation of the Romans with the
more distant princes, who felt the weight of their name
before experiencing that of their arms, so it excited envy
and apprehension in those who had seen and felt their
arms, amongst whom were the Latins. And this jealousy
and fear were so powerful that not only the Latins, but also
the colonies which the Romans had established in Latium,
together with the Campanians, whose defence the Romans
had but a short time previously undertaken, conspired
together against the Romans. The Latins began the war in
the way we have shown that most wars are begun, not by
attacking the Romans, but by defending the Sidicians from
the Samnites, against whom the latter were making war
with the permission of the Romans. And that it is true that
the Latins began the war because they had at last become
aware of the bad faith of the Romans is demonstrated by
Titus Livius, when at an assembly of the Latin people he
put the following words into the mouth of Annius Setinus, a
Latin Praetor: "For if now we can bear servitude under the
specious name of equal confederates", &c.

We see therefore that the Romans in the early beginning
of their power already employed fraud, which it has ever
been necessary for those to practise who from small beginnings wish to rise to the highest degree of power; and then
it is the less censurable the more it is concealed, as was that
practised by the Romans.

Men Often Deceive Themselves in Believing That by Humility They Can Overcome Insolence

WE OFTEN *see that humility not only is of no service, but is actually hurtful, especially when employed towards insolent men, who from jealousy or some other motive have conceived a hatred against you.*

It can be very tempting to treat an insolent foe with humility in the expectation that he will be disarmed and will cease to attack—but it doesn't work. Insolence cannot be placated, for it finds weakness contemptible; it will twist humility into fuel for its overbearing, obnoxious ways.

175

Perhaps you have difficulty reconciling this observation with the recommendation in Desmond Morris' *The Naked Ape* that one should play the role of the whipped dog to escape the wrath of an aggressive antagonist. True, you may escape such immediate ire by eating humble pie, but this does not mean that your long-term position in an organization will not be unfortunately affected. Humility works best in one-time encounters with aggressors who are of no consequence to your career. But if you allow yourself to become the office doormat, don't complain about the footprints on your back. Moreover, it should be pointed out that the aggrieved party cited in *The Naked Ape* had no effective power. What else can you be but humble to a traffic cop?

A realistic power base must be prepared to deal with insolence. Firmness and confidence in your position are the best defenses against insolent subordinates who are sometimes cowed by superiority, power, or position. Lay it on them if you have it and it suits your style.

Of this our historian gives proof on the occasion of the war between the Romans and Latins. For when the Samnites complained to the Romans that the Latins had attacked them, the Romans, unwilling to irritate the Latins, declined to forbid them to continue that war: This not only had the desired effect of not irritating them, but actually encouraged them to that degree that they almost immediately displayed open enmity towards the Romans. This appears from the words employed by the same Latin Praetor Annius, at the same assembly mentioned above, when he said: "You have put their patience to the proof in refusing them troops; who can doubt that this would have excited their resentment, and yet they have quietly borne this vexation. They have heard that we are arming against their allies the Samnites, and yet have not stirred from their city. Whence then comes their great modesty, but from their knowledge of our power and their own?" These words show in the clearest manner to what degree the patience of the Romans increased the insolence of the Latins. And therefore no prince should ever forego his rank, nor should he ever voluntarily give up anything (wishing to do so honorably) unless he is able or believes himself able to hold it. For it is almost always better (matters having come to the point that he cannot give it up in the above manner) to allow it to be taken from him by force, rather than by the apprehension of force. For if he yields it from fear, it is for the purpose of avoiding war, and he will rarely escape from that; for he to whom he has from cowardice conceded the one thing will not be satisfied, but will want to take other things from him, and his arrogance will increase as his esteem for the prince is lessened. And, on the other hand, the zeal of the prince's friends will be chilled on seeing him appear feeble or cowardly. But if, so soon as he discerns his adversary's intention, he prepares his forces, even though they be inferior, the enemy will begin to respect him, and the other neighboring princes will appreciate him the more; and seeing him armed for defence, those even will come to his aid who, seeing him give up himself, would never have assisted him.

This reasoning applies to the case when there is only one enemy; but when there are several, it will always be a wise plan for the prince to yield something of his possessions to some one of them, either for the purpose of gaining him over if war has already been declared, or to detach him from the enemies that are leagued against him.

Divide and conquer.

Feeble States Are Always Undecided in Their Resolves; and Slow Resolves Are Invariably Injurious

IN CONNECTION with this war between the Latins and the Romans, and its origin, we should observe that it is well in all deliberations to come at once to the essential point, and not always to remain in a state of indecision and uncertainty. This was evidenced in the council which the Latins held on the occasion when they contemplated detaching themselves from the Romans. For the Romans, being apprised of the evil disposition of the Latin people, wished to assure themselves upon that point, and to see whether they might regain their friendship without resorting to arms, and therefore requested the Latins to send eight of

179

their citizens to Rome for a conference. When the Latins were informed of this, conscious of having done many things that were displeasing to the Romans, they convoked a council to decide as to who should go to Rome, and to instruct them as to what they should say. And whilst discussing the matter, their Praetor Annius said these words: "I hold it to be of the highest importance for our interests that we should think rather of what we shall do than what we shall say; when we have decided upon that, it will be easy to accommodate our words to our acts."Certainly a most correct maxim, and one that should be borne in mind by all princes and republics; for it is impossible to explain one's self properly when in doubt and indecision as to what is to be done; but once resolved and decided, it is easy to find suitable words. I have the more willingly remarked upon this point as I have often known such indecision to interfere with proper public action, to the detriment and shame of our republic. *And it will always happen that in doubtful cases, where prompt resolution is required, there will be this indecision when weak men have to deliberate and resolve. Slow and dilatory deliberations are not less injurious than indecision, especially when you have to decide in favor of an ally; for tardiness helps no one and generally injures yourself.*

But how does this square with the advice given in the chapter of the First Book of *The Discourses,* which urges the administrator to "temporize" with an evil? Isn't that just a fancy way of saying that one should be slow in making a decision? I did not agree with Machiavelli's "temporizing" advice, so I find this advice more acceptable and even offer it in support of my previous position. Business executives have emphasized this facet of leadership almost universally:

The manager must make decisions. Indecisiveness is a weakness that can disable the administrator.

A government organization had budgeted $190,000 to equip a new operation. Funds not spent within two years reverted to the treasury. The administrator chose to spend the money by committee, thereby removing himself from the direct responsibility of purchasing the equipment. "Let the people buy what they want. If I buy it, there will be no end to the bitching!"

His argument had merit, but it also produced chaos. At the end of the first year, only $80,000 had been spent; many work units were without equipment, and the equipment that had been purchased had not been well received. Since this was a situation in which some people were bound to be displeased no matter what the results were, the administrator should have made the decisions himself or delegated the decision-making responsibility to another individual. As it was, decisions were delayed to the detriment of all. Committees are not renowned for their decision-making skills.

And the matter of allies is not to be overlooked. Your hesitation in making a decision favorable to an ally—a friend—tells him a great deal. If you are going to do something for a friend, then to hesitate robs you of his good will: He then knows the limits of your affection. If you dillydally with him and then turn him down, he will not think any more of you than if you had refused his request immediately—and perhaps less.

A foreman was having difficulty with one of his men who felt work rules were made for others. The man had been warned many times. One day his drinking on the job played a role in a shop accident. The foreman needed the general manager's approval to fire the man, so he laid out what he considered to be a cold case before the boss. He expected to hear, "Fire him!" Instead, he heard, "I'll think about it." The man continued working while the boss thought. And the boss

never knew why his foremen had so little control over the men and why the men had so little regard for the shop rules.

It ordinarily arises from lack of courage or force, or from the evil disposition of those who have to deliberate, being influenced by passion to ruin the state or to serve some personal interests, and who therefore do not allow the deliberations to proceed, but thwart and impede them in every way. Good citizens therefore never impede deliberations, especially in matters that admit of no delay, even if they see the popular impulse tending to a dangerous course.

How Often the Judgments of Men in Important Matters Are Erroneous

THOSE *who have been present at any deliberative assemblies of men will have observed how erroneous their opinions often are; and in fact, unless they are directed by superior men, they are apt to be contrary to all reason.*

It would seem that our legislatures and councils only offer more proof of this truth. Perhaps boards of directors should also be included in this category, for their record is not particularly impressive. More than a few investors and bankers have asked, "What was Penn Central's board doing all that time?" The an-

183

swer is quite simple: They were rubber stamping management's rush to bankruptcy. Robert Townsend, in his book *Up the Organization,* claimed that in his years as president he did not hear one useful comment from his board. To say that he is unimpressed with the ability of a board of directors to guide a firm's fortunes would be a gross understatement.

But as superior men in corrupt republics (especially in periods of peace and quiet) are generally hated, either from jealousy or the ambition of others, it follows that the preference is given to what common error approves, or to what is suggested by men who are more desirous of pleasing the masses than of promoting the general good. *When, however, adversity comes, then the error is discovered, and then the people fly for safety to those whom in prosperity they had neglected, as we shall show at length in its proper place.*

I am not at all certain that this is so. It would seem that people more frequently fly into the arms of the demagogues who promise them relief from whatever plagues them. The problem is that the people have no way of determining the wisdom of a man except by the noises he makes. If he makes the right noises, he's their man—regardless of his wisdom or abilities. Of course, one could counter with the Churchill epic for it certainly fits the Machiavellian model: Churchill's thoughts and talents were rejected in peacetime, but his leadership was sought in adversity.

Certain events also easily mislead men who have not a great deal of experience, for they have in them so much that resembles truth that men easily persuade themselves that they are correct in the judgment they have formed upon the subject.

The doctrine of infalliblity is not limited to the papacy; a great many of our political leaders and their critics have been persuaded that it also applies to them. The more a man knows, the more he thinks he knows—the arrogance of the "intellectual."

A famous chemist was not reluctant to express his contempt for business administrators. He felt he had been treated shabbily by a large chemical company for whom he had worked, and, after joining the academic world, he made no secret of his light regard for business administration education and its professors. Moreover, he felt the call to prove his mettle. He formed a company and persuaded some townspeople —who had come to accept his doctrine as gospel—to invest $500,000 in his enterprise.

The business professors had a field day: The chemist was "belly up" within a year. It was difficult to use his incredible blunders as classroom examples, for the students refused to believe that anyone could have been so stupid. Example: He built a 30,000-square-foot monument to his ego, only to learn what was meant by working capital; upon its completion, he was forced to sell his brick pile for a loss. And that was the least of his errors.

A wise man knows the true limits of his wisdom.

Contempt and Insults Engender Hatred Against Those Who Indulge in Them, Without Being of Any Advantage to Them

I HOLD it to be a proof of great prudence for men to abstain from threats and insulting words towards anyone, for neither the one nor the other in any way diminishes the strength of the enemy . . .

Never threaten! *Never!* If you mean to do something, don't talk about it—do it. If you're not going to do it, then don't say you will, for you may precipitate some action you will not relish.

Three men formed an industrial motion picture company. It prospered. Two of the men decided the third man was a waste of time, and they told him so; even more, they said they were going to vote him out of the presidency at the next stockholders' meeting. The man hopped on a plane and called on key stockholders to get their proxies. Two very surprised vice presidents at the meeting were given their walking papers. What purpose did their threat serve? Braggadocio! Ego balm! "We're going to show you!" Threats serve no constructive purpose. Rather, they give the advantage to the other party.

And what does an insult accomplish? Nothing, absolutely nothing! It certainly does not obtain the desired behavior from the insulted party; he will probably react adversely to it. Moreover, insults may fester and grow for years—and be avenged at a most inopportune time. The insulter is usually unaware that the revenge has been extracted.

An ill-tempered bar owner was prone to take his managerial frustrations out on his help by insulting them. One bartender found solace in tapping the till each time: $1 for a small insult; $5 for a stinging one.

Politeness pays dividends.

. . . but the one makes him more cautious, and the other increases his hatred of you, and makes him more persevering in his efforts to injure you. This was seen in the case of the Veienti . . . who added insulting words against the Romans to the injuries of war, which no prudent captain should permit his soldiers to indulge in, for they inflame and excite the enemy to revenge, and in no way impede his attacking you (as has been said), so that they are in fact so many weapons that will be turned against you. A striking instance of this occurred in Asia, when Gabades, commander of the Persians, having for a long time besieged Amida and becoming weary of the siege, resolved to abandon it;

and having already broken up his camp, the inhabitants of the place came upon the walls, and, inflated with the thought of victory, assailed his army with every kind of insult, vilifying them and accusing and reproaching them for their cowardice and poltroonery. Gabades, irritated by this, changed his mind and resumed the siege, and his indignation at these insults so stimulated his efforts, that he took the city in a few days and gave it up to sack and pillage. The same thing happened to the Veienti, who, not content with making war upon the Romans, outraged them with insulting words, advancing up to the very stockade of their camp to fling insults at them, thus irritating the Romans more by their words than their arms, so that the soldiers, who at first had fought unwillingly, now constrained the Consuls to bring on a battle, in which they made the Veienti suffer the penalties of their insolence. It is the duty, therefore, of every good general of an army, or chief of a republic, to use all proper means to prevent such insults and reproaches from being indulged in by citizens or soldiers, either amongst themselves or against the enemy for if used against an enemy they give rise to the above-described inconveniences, and between the soldiers and the citizens it is even worse, unless they are promptly put a stop to, as has ever been done by prudent rulers. The Roman legion that had been left at Capua, having conspired against the Capuans (as we shall relate in its place), and this conspiracy having given rise to a sedition which was quelled by Valerius Corvinus, one of the stipulations of the convention that was concluded with them provided the severest penalties against whoever should at any time reproach the soldiers with this selection. Tiberius Gracchus, who in the war with Hannibal had been called to the command of a certain number of slaves, who had been armed because of the scarcity of freemen, ordered amongst the first things that the penalty of death should be inflicted upon whoever reproached any of them with their former servitude; so dangerous did the Romans esteem it to treat men with contempt, or to reproach them with any previous disgrace, because nothing is more irritating and calculated to excited greater indignation than such reproaches, *whether founded upon truth or not; "for harsh sarcasms, even if they have but the least truth in them, leave their bitterness rankling in the memory."*

Wise Princes and Republics Should Content Themselves with Victory; for When They Aim at More, They Generally Lose

THE USE of insulting language towards an enemy arises generally from the insolence of victory, or from *the false hope of victory*, which latter misleads men as often in their actions as in their words; for when this false hope takes possession of the mind, it makes men go beyond the mark, and *causes them often to sacrifice a certain good for an uncertain better.*

Rare is the gambler who knows when to grab his winnings and run. He wins and wants more. It's called greed, but people can be greedy about things other

191

than money. Any victory sows the seeds of desire for an even larger victory, and, in pressing for it, victory can be lost. Many small entrepreneurs, whose enterprises have prospered, tried to expand rapidly—too rapidly—to "take advantage" of their good fortune, only to lose their whole operation when the expansion reaped losses.

One young man had a bit of good fortune building apartment houses, so he expanded rapidly into all types of commercial construction. At the peak of his career, he even bought a professional athletic team that played something resembling football. But he was grossly overextended by that time, and his empire collapsed in ruin.

And as this matter well merits consideration, it seems to me better to demonstrate it by ancient and modern examples, rather than attempt to do so by arguments, which will not do as well. After Hannibal had defeated the Romans at Cannae, he sent messengers to Carthage to announce his victory and to ask for support. The question as to what should be done was warmly discussed in the Senate of Carthage. Hanno, an old and sagacious citizen, advised that they should prudently avail of the victory to make peace with the Romans, which, he argued, they could do now with much more favorable conditions, having been victorious, than they could possibly have expected if they had been defeated; and that the object of the Carthaginians should be to show to the Romans that, whilst they were able to combat them, yet having won a victory they were not disposed to risk losing the fruits of it by the hope of still further successes. The Carthaginian Senate did not adopt this course, though they recognized the wisdom of it after the opportunity was lost. After Alexander the Great had conquered the entire Orient, the republic of Tyre (most eminent and powerful in those days, the city being situated upon the water like that of the Venetians) seeing the success and power of Alexander, sent ambassadors to him to assure him of their friendly disposition, and of their readiness to render him obedience, but that they could not consent to receive him or his forces within their city. Whereupon Alexander became indignant that a city should attempt to close her gates to him when all the rest of the world had thrown open theirs; he declined to receive the ambassadors, and, refusing the terms offered to him, he began to lay siege to the city. Tyre being surrounded by water, and abundantly supplied with provisions and all munitions necessary for her defence, Alexander found after four months of siege that the taking of the city would require more of his time and glory than most of his other conquests had done, and therefore resolved to try negotiations and to concede to the Tyrians all they themselves had asked. But the Tyrians on their part, having become elated, now refused to make terms, and killed the messengers whom Alexander had sent to them. This so enraged Alexander that he assaulted the city with such vigor that he captured and destroyed her, and made slaves of her men. In the year 1502 a Spanish army came into the Florentine dominions for the purpose of reinstating the Medici in the government of Florence, and to levy contributions from the city; the Spaniards had been called there by the citizens themselves, who had encouraged them with the hope that they would take up arms in their favor so soon as they should have entered the Florentine territory. But when the Spaniards had arrived in the plains of Florence, they found no one coming to their support, and having run out of provisions they attempted to open negotiations; but the citizens of Florence had become insolent and declined all terms. The loss of Prato and the ruin of their own state were the consequence of this conduct. Princes that are attacked cannot then commit a greater error, especially when their assailant greatly exceeds them in power, than to refuse all accommodation, and more particularly when it has been offered; for no terms will ever be so hard but what they will afford some advantage to him who accepts them, so that he really obtains thereby a share of the victory. And therefore the people of Tyre should have been satisfied to have Alexander accept the propositions which he had at first refused; for it would have been victory enough for them to have made so great a conqueror, with arms in hand come to their own terms. And so it should also have sufficed the Florentines, and it would have been a great victory for them, if the Spaniards had yielded in something to their will, without accomplishing all their own designs, which had for their object to change the government of Florence, to detach it from France, and to levy contributions from it. If out of these three objects the Spaniards had gained two, leaving to the people of Florence the first, namely its government, it would have been to some extent an honorable and satisfactory arrangement for both parties, and the people ought not to have cared about the two last points provided they preserved their liberty; nor should they (even if they had seen a chance of a greater and almost certain victory) have exposed their independence to the hazards of fortune, because that was their last stake, which no prudent man will ever risk except from extreme necessity.

Hannibal left Italy after sixteen years of triumphs, having been recalled by the Carthaginians to come to the rescue of his own country; he found Asdrubal and Syphax utterly beaten, the kingdom of Numidia lost, Carthage confined to the limits of her walls, and having no other resources to look to but him and his army. Knowing that this was the last resource of his country, Hannibal did not want to risk it without having first tried all other means, and was not ashamed to ask for peace, convinced that peace and not war was the only means of saving his country, The Romans having refused his request, he resolved to fight, though almost certain of defeat, judging that there might possibly be a chance of his being victorious, and that at least he should lose gloriously. And if so great and valiant a general as Hannibal, with his entire army, sought peace rather than risk a battle, seeing that his defeat would expose his country to enslavement, what should any less valiant and experienced generals do? But men always commit the error of not knowing where to limit their hopes, and by trusting to these rather than to a just measure of their resources, they are generally ruined.

How Dangerous It Is for a Republic or a Prince Not to Avenge a Public or a Private Injury

WHAT MEN will do from indignation and resentment is clearly seen from what happened to the Romans when they had sent the three Fabii as ambassadors to the Gauls, who had come to attack the Tuscans, and more especially the city of Clusium. The inhabitants having sent to Rome for assistance, the Romans sent ambassadors to the Gauls to notify them to abstain from making war upon their allies, the Tuscans. These ambassadors being more accustomed to act than to speak, and having arrived at the place at the very monent when the Tuscans and Gauls were engaged in battle, threw themselves upon the latter to combat them.

Having been recognized by these, all the resentment which before they had felt towards Tuscans was now turned against the Romans; and was increased even, because the Gauls complained through their ambassadors to the Romans of this wrong, and having demanded as a reparation therefore that the three Fabii should be delivered up to them, the Romans not only did not surrender or punish them in any way, but at the next assembling of the Comitii they were made Tribunes with consular powers. When the Gauls saw the very men who should have been chastised thus rewarded with honors, they regarded it as an intentional insult and disgrace to themselves; and, exasperated by anger and indignation, they attacked Rome and captured the whole city, excepting only the Capitol. This misfortune was brought upon themselves by the Romans, through nothing but their disregard of justice, and because their ambassadors, who had violated the laws of nations, instead of being punished, had been rewarded with high honors.

This shows how careful republics and princes should be to avoid similar wrongs, either to an entire people or to an individual; *for if any man be grievously wronged*, either by a state or by another individual, and satisfactory reparation be not made to him, if he lives in a republic *he will revenge himself, even if it involves the ruin of the state, and if he lives under a prince and be at all high-spirited, he will never rest until he have revenged himself upon him in some way, though he may see that it will cause his own ruin.*

The thirst for revenge is often unquenchable. It can fester, awaiting an opportunity to be satisfied, or it can explode in unreasonable, self-destructive fury. Inter-

nal Revenue Service files are replete with cases of disgruntled employees who sought revenge upon their employers by informing the government of discrepancies between the employer's tax returns and the truth. In his penchant for revenge, the informer may even implicate himself. But what can an administrator do to avoid revenge, aside from behaving in a manner that will not provoke it? In olden times, exile was one remedy: The injured party was physically removed from a position where revenge was feasible.

Don't give the aggrieved party easy weapons with which to seek revenge. Make him work hard for it. One indiscreet businessman allowed his bookkeeper to become aware of his habit of pocketing $20 from each day's cash intake without informing Uncle Sam of the transaction. In time, the bookkeeper came to see the advantages of the businessman's twilight dividends and decided to declare a few for himself. When the businessman discovered he had a partner, he dissolved the partnership with a few sharp comments. The word "thief" seemed to dominate the stormy exit interview; the employer was on the verge of calling the police when the bookkeeper suggested that his one phone call would be to the IRS fraud squad. Their joint enterprise ended with no severance pay, no recommendation, and lots of ill feelings. A few days later, the business man received a call from another firm asking for information about the departed till tapper. The businessman pulled no punches. His statements were so startling that the caller's curiosity forced him to drop a hint about the results of the investigation to the unemployed bookkeeper to see his reaction, which was, "I didn't think the old buzzard would be so stupid!" As he left, he headed for the phone booth and the ear of guess who.

To prove the truth of this, we have a most flagrant and authentic instance in the case of Philip of Macedon, father of Alexander the Great. Amongst the followers of his court was Pausanias, a noble youth of rare beauty, of whom Attalus, one of the chief officers of Philip, had become greatly enamored; and having several times pressed Pausanias to yield to his unnatural desires, which the youth had indignantly repelled, Attalus resolved by perfidy and force to obtain what he could not have otherwise. He therefore gave a grand banquet, to which he invited Pausanias, amongst a number of other nobles. After all had feasted and were filled with wine, he had Pausanias seized and carried to a retired place; and after having vented his own unnatural lust upon him, by way of subjecting him to still greater shame he caused a number of his other guests to subject him to a similar abuse. Pausanias repeatedly complained to Philip of this outrage, who for a while indulged him with the promise of revenge; but he not only failed to perform it, but promoted Attalus to the governorship of one of the Greek provinces. Whereupon Pausanias, seeing his enemy honored instead of being chastised, turned his whole resentment from him who had wronged him against Philip, for not having avenged him; and one morning, on the solemn occasion of the nuptials of the daughter of Philip with Alexander of Epirus, whilst Philip, accompanied by the two Alexanders, his son and son-in-law, was on his way to the temple to celebrate the marriage of his daughter, Pausanias slew him. This example, very similar to that of the Romans, should make all rulers remember never to esteem a man so lightly as to believe that, having heaped injuries and insults upon him, he will not seek to revenge himself, even at the risk of his own life.

How Dangerous It Is to Trust to the Representations of Exiles

IT SEEMS to me not amiss to speak here of the danger of trusting to the representations of men who have been expelled from their country, this being a matter that all those who govern states have to act upon almost daily; and I touch upon it the more willingly, as Titus Livius gives a most memorable instance of it, though in a measure foreign to the subject he treats upon. When Alexander the Great went with his army into Asia, Alexander of Epirus, his brother-in-law and uncle, came with his army into Italy, having been called there by the banished Lucanians, who had held out the hope to him that by their means he would be able to seize that whole country; and when Alexander, upon their assurances and the hopes held out by them, had come into Italy, they killed him, because they had been promised by the citizens of Lucania permission to return to their homes if they would assassinate Alexander. We see, then, how vain the faith and promises of men are who are exiles from their own country. As to their faith, we have to bear in mind that *whenever they can return to their country by other means than your assistance, they will abandon you and look to the other means, regardless of their promises to you. And as to their vain hopes and promises, such is their extreme desire to return to their homes that they naturally believe many things that are not true, and add many others on purpose; so that, with what they really believe and what they say they believe, they will fill you with hopes to that degree that if you attempt to act upon them you will incur a fruitless expense or engage in an undertaking that will involve you in ruin.*

Consider the Cuban exiles. What tales did they weave to the CIA to gain support for their counterrevolution? Exiles are selling a bill of goods. They want to justify the injustice of their exile in your eyes to gain your suppo45 while seeking revenge for their plight. They want sympathy, and thus will say whatever can elicit it. Their tales cannot always be regarded as factual.

Competitors' ex-employees can pose the same problems. They are exiles of a sort who may be tempted to paint inaccurate pictures of their former employers to justify their departures. Seldom do they perceive the truth. Many people fail to realize they were really fired and that their perceptions of management aptitude may therefore be somewhat distorted.

When an exile complains, "They never told me anything; they keep their people in the dark," it may merely be a reflection of his status as an outcast in the work

group. Outcasts usually have things to say that would
be denied by people in the work group. The wise exile
watches his tongue carefully, for he knows his plaints
may only injure his own image.

The example of Alexander of Epirus, just cited, will
suffice to prove the truth of this; but I will add that of
Themistocles the Athenian, who, having been declared a
rebel, fled to Darius in Asia, and made such representations and promises to him if he would attack Greece, that
Darius allowed himself to be persuaded to undertake it.
But when Themistocles found that he could not fulfil those
promises, he poisoned himself, either from shame or from
the fear of punishment. And if so eminent a man as Themistocles could commit so great an error, we may judge to
what extent men of less virtue allow themselves to be
misled by their desires and their passions. *A prince therefore should be slow in undertaking any enterprise upon the
representations of exiles, for he will generally gain nothing
by it but shame and serious injury.*

A merchant hired a young man who had been working
for a direct competitor until they came to an unpleasant
parting of the ways. The new employee filled his boss'
ears with wondrous tales about the salability of certain
lines of merchandise carried exclusively by the competitor, urging his new boss to take those lines away
from the other merchant. Finally, the merchant managed to woo two of his competitor's "prize" lines away
from him. Not only were the results disappointing, but
the retaliation was unpleasant. Spite is not only an ugly
motive; it can also be an expensive one.

The Discourses
Third Book

It May at Times Be the Highest Wisdom to Simulate Folly

NO ONE ever displayed so much sagacity, or was esteemed so wise on account of any distinguished act, as Junius Brutus deserves to be esteemed for his simulation of folly. And although Titus Livius gives but one reason that induced him to this simulation, namely, that he might live in greater security and preserve his patrimony, yet if we well consider his conduct we are led to believe that he had another reason, which was that by thus avoiding observation he would have a better chance of destroying the kings, and of liberating his country, whenever an opportunity should offer. And that such was really his thought may be seen, first, from his interpretation of the oracle of Apollo, when he pretended to have fallen and kissed the earth, hoping thereby to propitiate the gods to his projects; and afterwards, when on the occasion of the death of Lucretia, in the midst of the father, husband, and other relatives, he was the first to pluck the dagger from her breast and to make all present swear henceforth to suffer no king to reign in Rome.

All those who are dissatisfied with their ruler should take a lesson from this example of Brutus; they should measure and weigh well their strength, and if sufficently powerful to be able to declare themselves his enemies, and to make open war against the prince, then they should take that course as the least dangerous and most honorable. But if their condition be such that their forces do not suffice for open war against the prince, then they should seek by every art to win his friendship, and for this purpose employ all possible means, such as adopting his tastes, and taking delight in all things that give him pleasure. Such intimacy will insure you tranquillity without any danger, and enable you to share the enjoyment of the prince's good fortune with him, and at the same time afford you every convenience for satisfying your resentment. True, some people say that one should not keep so close to princes as to be involved in their ruin, nor so far away but what in case of their ruin you might thereby advance your own fortunes. This middle course would undoubtedly be the best to pursue, but as I believe that impossible, one of the above-described modes must be adopted—either to go away from them entirely, or to attach yourself very closely to them; and whoever attempts any other way, even though he be a personage of distinction, exposes himself to constant danger. Nor will it do for him to say, "I do not care for anything; I desire neither honor nor profit; all I want is to

live quietly and without trouble"—for such excuses would
not be admitted. Men of condition cannot choose their way
of living, and even if they did choose it sincerely and
without ambition, they would not be believed; and were
they to attempt to adhere to it, they would not be allowed
to do so by others.

It is advisable then at times to *feign folly,* as Brutus did;
and *this is sufficiently done by praising, speaking, seeing,
and doing things contrary to your way of thinking . . . and
merely to please the prince.*

The translation of Machiavelli's word into the English
word "folly" seems questionable, for careful reading
indicates a meaning other than that which we usually
ascribe to it. Perhaps it might be more accurate to say
that Machiavelli believed that at times it is wise to say
things and do things that your wisdom and good judgment tell you are wrong in order to stay close to the
seat of power and thereby keep yourself in a position to
take advantage of any opportunity that presents itself.

Subordinates in most organizations are so adept at
this skill that it is second nature to them. Some people
call them "yes-men"; others merely term them agree-
able. Whatever, one is not apt to stay close to power by
making noises contrary to the designs of the leader. It
takes a clever man indeed to counter the wishes of his
leader successfully

Earlier, Machiavelli voiced the opinion that a person
should stay close to power, rather than flee from it in
the hope that he will be recalled when the existing
leadership falters. Observation makes me wary of ac-
cepting this advice without question, for I have seen
several instances in which people were recalled to
power from afar. Moreover, people connected with a
discredited administration are seldom allowed to play

a role in the succeeding administration, no matter what their true attitudes or abilities are.

When it was discovered that one young football coach, who had led his team to fame, had bent a few NCAA rules, his university was penalized and most of his first- and second-string players were declared ineligible. The administration fired him. One of the several outstanding assistant coaches on his staff had been cleared of any participation in the previous illegal practices. The general consensus was that this assistant should be made head coach, and it was so recommended by the athletic committee. But the president would have no part of it; the whole staff had to go—guilty or not.

In a more typical changeover of power, lieutenants are often so jealous of one another or harbor so many resentments from previous injuries that they effectively block the promotion of one of their own number. The lieutenant who is supported by his peers is either a man of rare talent or someone the others do not fear—either because they own him or because he is harmless.

A Prince Cannot Live Securely in a State So Long as Those Live Whom He Has Deprived of It

THE ASSASSINATION of Tarquinius Priscus by the sons of Ancus, and the death of Servius Tullus caused by Tarquinius Superbus, prove *how difficult and dangerous it is to deprive anyone of a kingdom and leave him his life, even though you try to conciliate him by benefits.*

And how many ousted corporate leaders are left around the organization, perhaps as chairman of the board, awaiting reinstatement to power upon the failure of their successors? An article in *Business Week,* October 2, 1971, relates numerous tales of such former leaders still standing in the wings, interfering with the governmental reigns. But these are well-intentioned men, sometimes deprived of their former positions by their own initiative. What about those men who are really hurt but who are allowed to remain? There are many such men in the academic world because of tenure. A president, dean, or department head is dealt with harshly—or so he believes—but remains on the faculty.

One such demoted dean began a campaign of harassment against the administration, which caused serious problems, as the former dean had a great deal of support among certain segments of the faculty. He played a role in pulling down one administration and caused the following one some discomfort, but he had lost what support he had by the time he went to work on the third administration. Held in campuswide contempt, he garnered no support for his maneuvers. Such men owe it to themselves to clear out. Seldom does any good come from such situations.

We see how Tarquinius Priscus was deceived by the seemingly lawful possession of the sovereignty of Rome, which had been bestowed upon him by the people and confirmed by the Senate. He could not believe that resentment would so master the sons of Ancus that they would not be satisfied to submit to him, to whom all Rome yielded obedience. Servius Tullus in like manner deceived himself in supposing that he could win the sons of Tarquin with benefits. Thus the first may serve as a warning to all princes that they will never be safe so long as those live whom they have deprived of their possessions; and as to the second, it should remind every potenate that *old injuries can never be cancelled by new benefits, and the less so when the benefits are small in proportion to the injury inflicted.*

An obvious and important principle that the administrator should remember. It is unwise to allow a person who has been injured by you to remain in a position from which he can avenge himself. But everyone carries scars of former injuries and yet, because of the realities of the situation, must continue to function with the people responsible for those scars lest even greater injuries be inflicted.

To resolve this injury/benefit equation, an individual must balance the severity of the injury against the value of the benefit modified by the options that are open to him. Sometimes a person has no reasonable alternative but to accept whatever benefits he can get and take the accompanying injuries in stride. But be warned that, in such cases, he will probably seek revenge if given the opportunity.

Certainly Servius Tullus showed little sagacity when he supposed that the sons of Tarquin would remain content to be the sons-in-law of him whose kings they felt themselves entitled to be. And this desire to reign is so powerful that it not only dominates the minds of those born with the expectation of the throne, but also that of those who have no such expectations. This was well illustrated by the wife of Tarquin the younger, daughter of Servius, who urged on by this mad desire, regardless of all filial piety, stirred up her husband to deprive her father of his life and kingdom; so much more did she value being a queen than being the daughter of a king. If, then, Tarquinius Priscus and Servius

Tullus lost the kingdom from not knowing how to assure themselves of those whose thrones they had usurped, Tarquinius Superbus lost it by a disregard of the laws established by his predecessor.

Of Conspiracies

SOME MORE about conspiracies! Niccolò was concerned about them—and for good reason—so let's discuss them further.

It seems to me proper now to treat of conspiracies, being a matter of so much danger both to princes and subjects; for history teaches us that many more princes have lost their lives and their states by conspiracies than by open war. But *few can venture to make open war upon their sovereign, whilst everyone may engage in conspiracies against him.*

Everyone conspires to some degree. It is a universal human trait. A bit of thought about your relationships with large organizations will disclose the myriad of conspiracies which enable people to live with stifling regulations and cloddish management.

Universities fester as faculties conspire to outwit the regents' and top administrators' efforts to control their behavior: their office hours, teaching loads, class attendance, consultations. Administrations are helpless in the face of such widespread conspiracies. Conspiracy is a valid tactic, but I won't detail its workings—trade secrets, you know.

On the other hand, subjects cannot undertake more perilous and foolhardy enterprises than *conspiracies,* which are in every respect most difficult and dangerous; and thence it is that *though so often attempted, yet they so rarely attain the desired object.*

Not so! Machiavelli even said as much in the previous paragraph: "more princes have lost their lives and their states by conspiracies than by open war." It is a matter of the size and significance of the conspiracy. Small conspiracies usually succeed because the administrator is seldom aware of them; if he is, he may deem it best to ignore them for fear of becoming a "Captain Queeg." A management theorist might claim that small conspiracies within an organization may act as a lubricant, allowing the work group to function more efficiently in face of inhibiting regulations.

With its customary blundering, the legislature of one state has encumbered its college system with so many unworkable limitations that the institutions would be unable to function with any reasonable facility without the multitude of conspiracies that are perpetrated to evade the restrictions. Example: Funds for potential faculty members to visit campuses are practically unavailable because the legislature does not believe the state should pick up such tabs. But the realities of the situation dictate that if one desires to hire good men he must be prepared to pay such costs. You can't always build good faculties by hiring the local talent. Thus the colleges quietly bring in potential professors, calling them "lecturers" and paying their costs from that more generous budget. The supply budget is generous, but the equipment budget is almost nonexistent. It's amazing what can be called a supply.

If all this duplicity offends some people, bear in mind that it is to one purpose: to do the best job that can be done under the circumstances. Thus, conspiracies may serve good purposes as well as bad.

And therefore, so that princes may learn to guard against such dangers, and that subjects may less rashly engage in them, and learn rather to live contentedly under such a government as Fate may have assigned to them. . .

This statement is not calculated to win the favor of many moderns. Yet think a bit! Perhaps Niccolò is trying to provide one key to happiness. Observation leads to the conclusion that people who are in continual conflict with their government, habitual criminals, are seldom very happy people nor do they seem to lead very fruitful lives.

. . . I shall treat the subject at length, and endeavor not to omit any point that may be useful to the one or the other. And certainly that is a golden sentence of Cornelius Tacitus, where he says "that men should honor the past and obey the present; and whilst they should desire good princes, they should *bear with those they have, such as they are"—and surely whoever acts otherwise will generally involve himself and his country in ruin.*

In entering upon the subject, then, we must consider first against whom conspiracies are formed; and it will be found generally that they are made either against the country or against the prince.

> Or conspiracies can be made against the rules. Men may be satisfied with their organization or country but conspire to evade its rules.

It is of these two kinds that I shall speak at present; for conspiracies that have for their object the surrender of any town to an enemy that besieges it, or that have some similar purpose, have already been sufficiently discussed above. In the first instance, we will treat of those that are aimed against the sovereign, and examine the causes that provoke them; these are many, though one is more important than all the rest, namely, *his being hated by the mass of the people.* For when a prince has drawn upon himself universal hatred, it is reasonable to suppose that there are some particular individuals whom he has injured more than others, and who therefore desire to revenge themselves. This *desire is increased by seeing the prince held in general aversion.* A prince, then, should avoid incurring such universal hatred; and, as I have spoken elsewhere of the way to do this, I will say no more about it here. If the prince will avoid this general hatred, the particular wrongs to individuals will prove less dangerous to him; partly because men rarely attach sufficient importance to any

wrong done them to expose themselves to great danger for
the sake of avenging it, and partly because, even if they
were so disposed and had the power to attempt it, *they
would be restrained by the general affection for the prince.*
The different wrongs which a prince can inflict upon a
subject consist either in an attempt upon *his possessions,
his person, or his honor.* In matter of personal injury,
threats are worse than the execution; in fact, menaces
involve the only danger, there being none in the execution, for the dead cannot avenge themselves, and in most
cases the survivors allow the thought of revenge, to be
interred with the dead. But he who is threatened and sees
himself constrained by neccessity either to dare and do or
to suffer becomes a most dangerous man to the prince as we
shall show in its proper place. Besides this kind of injury a
*man's property and honor are the points upon which he will
be most keenly sensitive.* A prince, then, should be most
careful to avoid touching these; for he can never despoil a
man so completely but what he will cherish a determined
desire for revenge. As to attacking men's honor, that of
their wives is what they feel most, and after that their being
themselves treated with indignity. . . .

There is another and still more powerful motive that
makes men conspire against their princes, and that is the
desire to liberate their country from the tyranny to which it
has been subjected by the prince. It was this that stirred up
Brutus and Cassius against Caesar; it was this that excited
others against the Falari, the Dionysii, and other usurpers.
And no tyrant can secure himself against such attacks,
except by voluntarily giving up his usurpation. But as none
of them ever take this course, there are but few that do not
come to a bad end. . . .

The perils incurred by conspirators are great . . . because they present themselves at every moment. There is danger in plotting and in the execution of the plot, and even after it has been carried into effect. A plot may be formed by a single individual or by many; the one cannot be called a conspiracy, but rather a determined purpose on the part of one man to assassinate the prince. In such case, the first of the three dangers to which conspiracies are exposed is avoided; for the individual runs no risk before the execution of his plot, for as no one possesses his secret, there is no danger of his purpose coming to the ears of the prince. Any individual, of whatever condition, may form such a plot, be he great or small, noble or plebeian, familiar or not familiar with the prince; for everyone is permitted on occasions to speak to the prince, and has thus the opportunity of satisfying his vengeance. Pausanias, of whom I have spoken elsewhere, killed Philip of Macedon as he was proceeding to the temple, surrounded by a thousand armed men, and having his son and his son-in-law on either side. But Pausanias was a noble, and well known to the prince. A poor and abject Spaniard stabbed King Ferdinand of Spain in the neck; the wound was not mortal, but it showed nevertheless that this man had the audacity as well as the opportunity of striking the prince. . . . I believe it is not uncommon to find men who form such projects (the mere purpose involving neither danger nor punishment), but few carry them into effect; and of those who do, *very few or none escape being killed in the execution of their designs*, and therefore but few are willing to incur such certain death.

The history of the assassinations of the U.S. presidents seems to bear out Niccolò's thoughts. Most of the successful ones were evidently solo affairs, Lincoln being the exception.

But let us leave the plots formed by single individuals, and come to conspiracies formed by a number of persons. These, I say, have generally for their originators the great men of the state or those on terms of familiar intercourse with the prince. None other, unless they are madmen, can engage in conspiracies; for men of low condition, who are not intimate with the prince, have no chance of success, not having the necessary conveniences for the execution of their plots. In the first place, men of no position have not the means of assuring themselves of the good faith of their accomplices, as no one will engage in their plot without the hope of those advantages that prompt men to expose themselves to great dangers. And thus, so soon as they have drawn two or three others into their scheme, some one of them denounces and ruins them. But supposing even that they have the good fortune not to be betrayed, they are nevertheless exposed to so many difficulties in the execution of the plot, from being debarred free access to the prince, that it seems almost impossible for them to escape ruin in the execution. For if the great men of a state, who are in familiar intercourse with the prince, succumb under the many difficulties of which we have spoken, it is natural that these difficulties should be infinitely increased for the others. And therefore those who know themselves to be weak avoid them, for where men's lives and fortunes are at stake they are not all insane; and when they have cause for hating a prince, they content themselves with cursing and vilifying him, and wait until someone more powerful and of higher position than themselves shall avenge them. Still, if one of this class of persons should be daring enough to attempt such an undertaking, he would merit praise rather for his intention than for his prudence.

We see, then, that conspiracies have generally been set on foot by the great, or the friends of the prince; and of these, as many have been prompted to it by an excess of benefits as by an excess of wrongs. . . . And certainly if any conspiracy of the great against a prince is likely to succeed, it should be one that is headed by one, so to say, almost himself a king, who can afford the conspirators every opportunity to accomplish his design; but, blinded by the ambition of dominion, they are equally blind in the conduct of the conspiracy, for if their villainy were directed by prudence, they could not possibly fail of success. *A prince, then, who wishes to guard against conspiracies should fear those on whom he has heaped benefits quite as much, and even more, than those whom he has wronged.* . .

Interesting! Those close to power feel safer in their plotting, for they feel their cushion of good will and trust will cloak and protect them. An enemy knows he will be dealt with harshly upon discovery.

. . . for the latter lack the convenient opportunities which the former have in abundance. The intention of both is the same, for the thirst of dominion is as great as that of revenge, and even greater. A prince, therefore, should never bestow so much authority upon his friends but that there should always be a certain distance between them and himself, and that there should always be something left for them to desire; otherwise they will almost invariably become victims of their own imprudence, as happened to those whom we have mentioned above.

But to return to our subject. Having said that conspiracies are generally made by the great, who have free access to the prince, let us see now what their results have been, and what the causes were that influenced their success or their failure. As we have said above, there are in all

conspiracies three distinct periods of danger. The first is in
the organization of the plot, and as but few have a successful issue, it is impossible that all should pass happily
through this first stage, which presents the greatest dangers; and therefore I say that it requires the extremest
prudence, or great good fortune, that a conspiracy shall not
be discovered in the process of formation. Their discovery
is either by denunciation or by surmises. Denunciation is
the consequence of treachery or of want of prudence on the
part of those to whom you confide your designs; *and
treachery is so common that you cannot safely impart your
project to any but such of your most trusted friends as are
willing to risk their lives for your sake,* or to such other
malcontents as are equally desirous of the prince's ruin. Of
such reliable friends you may find one or two; but as you
are necessarily obliged to extend your confidence, it becomes impossible to find many such, for their devotion to
you must be greater than their sense of danger and fear of
punishment. Moreover, *men are very apt to deceive themselves as to the degree of attachment and devotion which
others have for them, and there are no means of ascertain-
ing this except by actual experience* . . .

> Egos have been shattered upon the discovery that
> "trusted friends" weren't to be trusted. Seldom will you
> have associates with whom you can safely undertake
> large conspiracies. If possible, one should so design
> his conspiracy that he has contingency plans in case of
> betrayal. Betrayal should never come as too much of a
> surprise.
>   Several men, after building a successful enterprise,
> fell to fighting over the booty. Two of the men had a
> very close working relationship, the older man having
> aided the younger man's career in a great many ways.

Time and again the younger man would proclaim for all to hear how he worshipped his sponsor. As the battle lines were drawn up in the enterprise and each side conspired against the other, the two men were together in the fray—together, that is, until it became apparent that they were holding the weaker hand, at which time the younger man silently sold out to the other side while still seeming to remain loyal to his sponsor.

. . . but experience in such matters is of the utmost danger. And even if you should have tested the fidelity of your friends on other occasions of danger, yet you cannot conclude from that that they will be equally true to you on an occasion that presents infinitely greater dangers than any other. If you attempt to measure a man's good faith by the discontent which he manifests towards the prince, you will be easily deceived, for by the very fact of communicating to him your designs, you give him the means of putting an end to his discontent; and to insure his fidelity, his hatred of the prince or your influence over him must be very great. It is thus that so many conspiracies have been revealed and crushed in their incipient stage; so that it may be regarded almost as a miracle when so important a secret is preserved by a number of conspirators for any length of time. . . . *When the number of accomplices in a conspiracy exceeds three or four, it is almost impossible for it not to be discovered, either through treason, imprudence, or carelessness.* The moment more than one of the conspirators is arrested, the whole plot is discovered; for it will be impossible for any two to agree perfectly as to all their statements. If only one be arrested, and he be a man of courage and firmness, he may be able to conceal the names of his accomplices; but then the others, to remain safe, must be equally firm, and not lay themselves open to discovery by flight, for if any one of them proves wanting in courage, whether it be the one that is arrested or one of those that are at liberty, the conspiracy is sure to be discovered. Titus Livius cites a very remarkable instance that occurred in connection with the conspiracy against Hieronymus, king of Syracuse. Theodorus, one of the conspirators, having been arrested, concealed with the utmost firmness the names of the other conspirators, and charged the matter upon the friends of the king; and, on the other hand, all the other conspirators had such confidence in the courage of Theodorus, that not one of them left Syracuse, or betrayed the least sign of fear. The conduct of a conspiracy then is exposed to all such dangers before it can be carried into execution; and to avoid these perils the following remedies present themselves. The first and most certain, I should rather say the only one, is *not to afford your associates in the plot any time to betray you;* and therefore *you should confide your project to them at the moment of its execution and not sooner.*

But this is seldom feasible in business.

Those who act thus are most likely to escape the first of the three dangers, and frequently also the others; and therefore have their enterprises almost always succeeded. And any man of prudence will always be able to govern himself in this wise.

I will cite two examples of this. Nelematus, unable to bear the tyranny of Aristotimus, tyrant of Epirus, assembled in his house a number of friends and relatives, and urged them to liberate their country from the yoke of the tyrant. Some of them asked for time to consider the matter, whereupon Nelematus made his slaves close the door of his house, and then said to those he had called together, "You must either go now and carry this plot into execution, or I shall hand you all over as prisoners to Aristotimus." Moved by these words, they took the oath demanded of them, and immediately went and carried the plot of Nelematus successfully into execution. A Magian having by craft usurped the throne of Persia, and the fraud having been discovered by Ortanus, one of the grandees of the realm, he conferred with six other princes of the state as to the means of ridding themselves of this usurper. When one of them inquired as to the time when they should act, Darius, one of the six assembled by Ortanus, arose and said, "We must either go now at this very moment and carry it into execution, or I shall go and denounce you all," whereupon they all arose, and, without affording any one time to repent, they carried their design into execution without difficulty. . . .

And thus, if we examine all the other instances, but few will be found where the conspirators might not have acted in the same way; but men not accustomed to the affairs of this world often commit the greatest mistakes, and especially in matters that are so much out of the ordinary course as conspiracies. *One should therefore never open himself on the subject of a conspiracy except under the most pressing necessity,* and only at the moment of its execution; and then only to one man, whose fidelity he has thoroughly tested for a long time, and who is animated by the same desire as himself. One such is much more easily found than many, and therefore there is much less danger in confiding your secret to him; and then, even if he were to attempt to betray you, there is some chance of your being able to defend yourself, which you cannot when there are many conspirators. I have heard many wise men say that you may talk freely with one man about everything, for unless you have committed yourself in writing the "yes" of one man is worth as much as "no" of another; therefore *one should guard most carefully against writing, as against a dangerous rock, for nothing will convict you quicker than your own handwriting.*

Amen! Letters, memos, anything in black and white. A young man and his lawyer conspired to hoodwink a man who was selling his business. While the business was technically being sold to the young man's corporation with nothing down on a ten-year note, he said that he would buy the note from the businessman personally. Once the sale was completed, the young man refused to buy the note, but his lawyer had written a letter to the seller's lawyer in which such an arrangement was mentioned in sufficient detail that it was deemed part of the contract. As the seller and his lawyer walked away from a successful meeting with their adversaries, the lawyer smiled and said, "I guess they forgot to tell him about writing letters in law school. He just learned about 'em!"

A businessman received a letter from a local concern saying that his name had been given as a reference by a certain job applicant with whom he was well acquainted both as a friend and a customer. His response was candid: He gave the good with the bad. The man was hired in spite of the letter, which on an overall basis was unfavorable. Later, he saw the letter in the firm's files. The businessman suspected the truth when this man took his business elsewhere and became quite distant.

There are two risks in communicating a plot to any one individual: the first, lest he should denounce you voluntarily; the second, lest he should denounce you, being himself arrested on suspicion, or from some indications, and being convicted and forced to it by the torture. But there are means of escaping both these dangers: the first, by denial and by alleging personal hatred to have prompted the accusation; and the other, by denying the charge, and alleging that your accuser was constrained by the force of torture to tell lies. But the most prudent course is not to communicate the plot to anyone, and to act in accordance with the above-cited examples; and if you cannot avoid drawing some one into your confidence, then to let it be not more than one, for in that case the danger is much less than if you confide in many.

Another necessity may force you to do unto the prince that which you see the prince about to do to you; the danger of which may be so pressing as not to afford you the time to provide for your own safety. Such a necessity ordinarily insures success, as the following two instances will suffice to prove. The Emperor Commodus had amongst his nearest friends and intimates Letus and Electus, two captains of the Praetorian soldiers; he also had Marcia as his favorite concubine. As these three had on several occasions reproved him for the excesses with which he had stained his own dignity and that of the Empire, he resolved to have them killed, and wrote a list of the names of Marcia, Letus, and Electus, and of some other persons, whom he wanted killed the following night. Having placed this list under his pillow, he went to the bath; a favorite child of his, who was playing in the chamber and on the bed, found this list, and on going out with it in his hand was met by Marcia, who took the list from the child. Having read it, she immediately sent for Letus and Electus, and when these three had thus become aware of the danger that threatened them, they resolved to forestall the

Emperor, and without losing any time they killed Commodus the following night. The Emperor Antonnius Caracalla was with his armies in Mesopotamia and had for his prefect Macrinus, a man more fit for civil than military matters. As is always the case with bad rulers, they are in constant fear lest others are conspiring to inflict upon them the punishment which they are conscious of deserving; thus Antoninus wrote to his friend Maternianus in Rome to consult the astrologers as to whether anyone was aspiring to the Empire and to advise him of it. Maternianus wrote back that Macrinus was thus aspiring, and this letter fell into the hands of Macrinus before it reached the Emperor. He at once directed his trusted friend, the Centurion Martialis, whose brother had been slain by Caracalla a few days before, to assassinate him, which he succeeded in doing. From this we see that the necessity which admits of no delay produces the same effect as the means employed by Nelematus in Epirus, of which I have spoken above. It also proves the truth of what I said in the beginning of this discourse, that to threaten is more dangerous for princes, and more frequently causes conspiracies, than the actual injury itself; and therefore princes should guard against indulging in menaces. For you must bind men to you by benefits, or you must make sure of them in some other way, *but never reduce them to the alternative of having either to destroy you or perish themselves.*

Conversely, always make sure the other person will lose something if he attacks you. The discharged employee is hopefully restained from doing a great many things that he would like to do through fear of what it might cost him in terms of pay, good recommendations, and the law.

Three men, who were partners in a most profitable enterprise, became separately enmeshed in another business venture that turned sour and threatened them all with bankruptcy. Two of the partners blamed the third for their troubles and demanded that he stand all of the loss. The third partner refused—although he could have afforded the loss more than the other two. The two threatened partners, deciding that it was either him or them, devised an elaborate but feasible plan to cover their losses from the third man's share of their profitable partnership.

Under normal circustances, the ousted partner would seek revenge; however, the two remaining partners provided that he be paid his remaining investment over a period of years. He was prevented from moving against the new partnership, for to do so would have resulted in the total loss of his investments.

As to the dangers that occur in the execution of a conspiracy, these result either from an unexpected change in the order of proceeding, or from the lack of courage in those who are charged with the execution of the plot, or from some error on their part, owing to want of foresight in leaving some of those alive whom it was intended to have killed. There is nothing that disturbs or impedes the actions of men more than when suddenly, and without time to reflect, the order of things agreed upon has to be entirely changed. And if such a change causes embarrassment in ordinary affairs, it does so to an infinitely greater degree in war or in conspiracies; for in such matters nothing is more essential than that men should firmly set their minds on performing the part that has been assigned to them. And if men have their minds fixed for some days upon a certain order and arrangement, and this be suddenly changed, it is impossible that this should not disturb them so as to defeat the whole plot. *So that it is much better to carry out any such project according to the original plan, even if it should present some inconveniences, rather than to change the order agreed upon and incur a thousand embarrassments.* And this will occur, if there be not time to reorganize the project entirely; for when there is time for that, men can suit themselves to the new order of things. . . .

Conspiracies against single individuals are generally apt to fail, for the reasons I have adduced; but when undertaken against two or more persons, they fail much easier. Such conspiracies present so many difficulties that it is almost impossible they should succeed. In fact, to strike two blows of this kind at the same instant and in different places is impracticable, and to attempt to do so at different moments of time would certainly result in the one's preventing the other. So that, if it is imprudent, rash, and doubtful to conspire against a single prince, it amounts to folly to do so against two at the same time. And were it not for the respect which I have for the historian, I should not be able to believe possible what Herodianus relates of Plautianus, when he charged the centurion Saturninus by himself to kill Severus and Caracalla, who lived separately in different places; for it is so far from being reasonable, that nothing less than the authority of Herodianus could make me believe it. Some young men of Athens conspired against Diocles and Hippias, tyrants of Athens; they succeeded in killing Diocles, but missed Hippias, who avenged him. Chion and Leonidas of Heraclea, disciples of Plato, conspired against the tyrants Clearchus and Satirus; they slew Clearchus, but Satirus, who remained, avenged him. The Pazzi, whom I have mentioned several times, succeeded only in killing Giuliano. Thus conspiracies against several persons at the same time should be avoided; they do no good to the conspirators, nor to the country, nor to anyone, but rather cause the tyrants that survive to become more cruel and insupportable than before, as was the case with those of Florence, Athens, and Heraclea, already mentioned above. It is true that the conspiracy of Pelopidas to deliver his country, Thebes, from her tyrants succeeded most happily, despite of all those obstacles; and he conspired not only against two, but against ten tyrants, and, so far from having ready access to them, he had been declared a rebel and had been banished. With all this, he was enabled to come to Thebes to slay the tyrants and free his country. But he succeeded thus mainly through the assistance of a certain Charon, privy counsellor of the tyrants, who facilitated his access to them and the consequent execution of his plot. Let no one, however, be seduced by this example; for it was an almost impossible enterprise, and its success was a marvel, and was so regarded by the historians, who speak of it as a most extraordinary and unprecedented event. The execution of such a plot may be interrupted by the least false alarm or by some unforeseen accident at the moment of its execution.

The morning of the day when Brutus and his fellow-conspirators intended to kill Caesar, it happened that the latter had a long conversation with Cn. Popilius Lena, one of the conspirators. This was observed by the other conspirators, who at once imagined that Popilius had denounced the conspiracy to Caesar and were tempted to assassinate Caesar on the spot, and not to wait until he should reach the Senate; and they would have done so, had they not observed that after the conversation Caesar made no extraordinary movement, which reassured them. These false apprehensions are not to be disregarded and should be carefully considered, the more so as it is very easy to be surprised by them; *for a man who has a guilty conscience readily thinks that everybody is speaking of him. You may overhear a word spoken to someone else that will greatly disturb you, because you think it has reference to you, and may cause you either to discover the conspiracy by flight or embarrass its execution by hastening it before the appointed time.* And this will happen the more easily the more accomplices there are in the conspiracy.

As to the unforeseen accidents, of course no idea can be given of them; they can only be illustrated by examples that should serve as a caution. Julio Belanti of Sienna (of whom I have already made mention) hated Pandolfo for having taken his daughter away from him after having first given her to him as his wife. He resolved to kill him, and thus chose his time. Pandolfo went almost daily to visit a sick relative, and in going there he passed before Julio's house, who, having observed it, arranged to have the conspirators there assassinate Pandolfo when he passed. He concealed them, well armed, behind the house door, whilst one of them was stationed at the window to watch for the coming of Pandolfo, and to give a signal when he should be near the door. Pandolfo came, and the signal was given by the conspirator at the window; but at that moment a friend met and stopped Pandolfo, whilst some who were with him moved on, and, upon hearing the noise of arms within the door of Julio, they discovered the ambush, so that Pandolfo was enabled to save himself, and Julio, with his accomplices, was obliged to fly from Sienna. This accidental meeting with a friend prevented the execution of the plot and thwarted the design of Julio. Such accidents, being rare, cannot be foreseen nor prevented; though one should endeavor to foresee all that can happen, so as to guard against it.

It only remains for us now to speak of the dangers that follow the execution of a plot; of which there is really but one, namely, when someone is left who will avenge the prince that is killed. He may have brothers or sons, or other relatives, who inherit the principality, and who have been spared by your negligence or for some of the reasons we have mentioned above, and who will avenge the prince. This happened to Giovan Andrea da Lampognano, who, together with other conspirators, had killed the Duke of Milan, who left a son and two brothers, who in time avenged the murdered Duke. But truly in such cases the conspirators are not to be blamed, because there is no help for it. There is no excuse for them however, when from want of foresight or negligence they permit any one to escape. Some conspirators of Furli killed the Count Girolamo, their lord, and took his wife and children, who were of tender age, prisoners. Believing, however, that they could not be secure if they did not obtain possession of the castle, which the castellan refused to surrender, the Lady Catharine, as the Countess was called, promised to the conspirators to procure its surrender if they would allow her to enter it, leaving them her children as hostages. Upon this pledge the conspirators consented to let her enter the castle; but no sooner was she within than she reproached them for the murder of the Count, and threatened them with every kind of vengeance. And to prove to them that she cared not for her children, she pointed to her sexual parts, calling out to them that she had wherewith to have more children. Thus the conspirators discovered their error too late, and suffered the penalty of their imprudence in perpetual exile. *But of all the perils that follow the execution of a conspiracy, none is more certain and none more to be feared than the attachment of the people to the prince that has been killed.*

Lincoln was never loved so much in life as he was in
death, and Kennedy worship runs unabated.

There is no remedy against this, for the conspirators can
never secure themselves against a whole people. As an
instance of this, I will cite the case of Julius Caesar, who,
being beloved by the people, was avenged by them; for
having driven the conspirators from Rome, they were the
cause of their being all killed at various times and places.

Conspiracies against the state are less dangerous for
those engaged in them than plots against the life of the
sovereign. In their conduct there is not so much danger, in
their execution there is the same, and after execution there
is none. In the conduct of the plot the danger is very slight,
for a citizen may aspire to supreme power without man-
ifesting his intentions to anyone; and if nothing interferes
with his plans, he may carry them through successfully, or
if they are thwarted by some law, he may await a more
favorable moment and attempt it by another way. This is
understood to apply to a republic that is already partially
corrupted; for in one not yet tainted by corruption such
thoughts could never enter the mind of any citizen. Citizens of a republic, then, may by a variety of ways and
means aspire to sovereign authority without incurring
great risks. If republics are slower than princes, they are
also less suspicious and therefore less cautious; and if they
show more respect to their great citizens, these in turn are
thereby made more daring and audacious in conspiring
against them.

Everybody has read the account written by Sallust of the
conspiracy of Catiline, and knows that, after it was discovered, Catiline not only stayed in Rome, but actually went
to the Senate, and said insulting things to the Senate and

the Consul; so great was the respect in which Rome held the citizens. And even after his departure from Rome, and when he was already with the army, Lentulus and the others would not have been seized if letters in their own handwriting had not been found, which manifestly convicted them. Hanno, one of the most powerful citizens of Carthage, aspired to the tyranny of the state, and arranged to poison the whole Senate on the occasion of his daughter's marriage, and then to make himself sovereign. When this plot was discovered, the Senate did nothing more than to pass a decree limiting the expense of feasts and weddings; such was the respect which the Carthaginians had for so great a citizen as Hanno.

It is true that in the execution of a conspiracy against one's country there are greater difficulties and dangers to surmount. For it is very rare that the forces of a conspirator suffice against so many; and it is not everyone that controls an army, like Caesar, or Agathocles, or Cleomenes, and the like, who by a single blow made themselves masters of their country. For such men the execution is sure and easy, but others who have not the support of such forces must employ deceit and cunning, or foreign aid.

As to the employment of deceit and cunning, I give the following instances. Pisistratus, after the victory which he had gained over the people of Megara, was greatly beloved by the people of Athens. One morning he went forth from his house wounded, and charged the nobility with having attacked him from jealousy, and demanded permission to keep a guard of armed followers for his protection, which was accorded him. This first step enabled him easily to attain such power that he soon after made himself tyrant of Athens. Pandolfo Petrucci returned with other exiles to Sienna, where he was appointed to the command of the guard of the government palace, a subordinate employ which others had refused. Nevertheless, this command gave him in time such influence and authority that in a little while he became prince of the state. Many others have employed similar means, and have, in a short time, and without danger, acquired sovereign power. Those who have conspired against their country with their own forces, or by the aid of foreign troops, have had various success, according to their fortune. Catiline, whose conspiracy we have already spoken of, succumbed. Hanno, whom we have also mentioned, having failed in his attempt with poison, armed his partisans to the number of many thousands, and perished with them. Some of the first citizens of Thebes, wishing to obtain absolute control of the state, called to their aid a Spartan army and seized the government. Thus, if we examine all the conspiracies attempted by men against their country, we find none, or but very few, that have failed in their conduct; but in their execution they have either met with success or failure. Once, however, carried into effect, they involve no other dangers but such as are inherent to absolute power; for he who has become a tyrant is exposed only to the natural and ordinary dangers which tyranny carries with it, and against which there are no other remedies than those indicated above.

Those are the considerations that have presented themselves to me in treating the subject of conspiracies; and if I have noted only those where the sword is the instrument employed, and not poison, it is because the course of both is absolutely the same. It is true that the latter are, in proportion, more dangerous, as their success is more uncertain, for it is not everyone that has the means of employing poison; it must, therefore, be intrusted to such as have, and that very necessity causes the dangers. Furthermore, many reasons may prevent a poison from proving mortal, as in the case of Commodus. Those who had conspired against him, seeing that he would not take the poisoned draught they had offered to him, and yet being resolved upon his death, were obliged to strangle him.

There is, then, no greater misfortune for a prince than that a conspiracy should be formed against him; for it either causes his death, or it dishonors him. If the conspiracy succeeds, he dies; if it be discovered, and he punishes the conspirators with death, it will always be believed that it was an invention of the prince to satisfy his cruelty and avarice with the blood and possessions of those whom he had put to death. I will, therefore, not omit offering an advice to princes or republics against whom conspiracies may have been formed. *If they discover that a conspiracy exists against them, they must, before punishing its authors, endeavor carefully to know its nature and extent—to weigh and measure well the means of the conspirators, and their own strength. And if they find it powerful and alarming, they must not expose it until they have provided themselves with sufficient force to crush it, as otherwise they will only hasten their own destruction. They should therefore try to simulate ignorance of it, for if the conspirators should find themselves discovered they will be forced by necessity to act without consideration.*

Now you understand why the government always investigates an assassination carefully to see if it was part of a conspiracy. If you discover conspirators, keep your cool until you can take care of them all.

A new branch manager of a business machines company instituted several changes that he felt were needed. His changes were not well received by several of the older salesmen, some of whom were very large producers. These men confronted the new manager with an ultimatum: "Rescind the orders or we will take our accounts to another employer."

The young manager answered, "I'll think about what you've said," and caught the next plane to the home office to discuss the situation with his superiors. He returned that night with a letter giving him the power to fire the whole crew, if he so desired. He kept it in his pocket, but told the salesmen that the new rules would stand. Then he sat back to await their action. They were bluffing. A real manager was born.

As an instance of this, we have the case of the Romans, who had left two legions at Capua to protect its inhabitants against the Samnites. The commanders of these legions (as we have related elsewhere) conspired to make themselves masters of the city. When this became known at Rome, the new Consul Rutilius was directed to see to its being prevented; and by way of lulling the conspirators into security, he published that the Senate had resolved to continue the legions in garrison at Capua. The captains and soldiers, believing this, and thinking, therefore, that they had ample time for the execution of their design, made no attempt to hasten it, and thus waited until they perceived that the Consul was separating them from each other. This excited their suspicions, and caused them to expose their intentions, and to proceed to the execution of their plot. There could not be a more forcible example than this for both parties; for it shows how dilatory men are when they think that they have time enough, and, on the other hand, how prompt they are in action when impelled by necessity. A prince or a republic who, for their own advantage, wish to defer the disclosure of a conspiracy, cannot use a more effectual means for that purpose than artfully to hold out to the conspirators the prospect of an early and favorable opportunity for action; so that, whilst waiting for that, or persuaded that they have ample time, the prince or republic will themselves gain time to overwhelm the conspirators. Those who act differently will accelerate their own ruin, as was the case with the Duke of Athens and Guglielmo de' Pazzi. The Duke, having become tyrant of Florence, and being apprised that there was a conspiracy on foot against him, had one of the conspirators seized without further inquiry into the matter. This caused the others at once to take to arms, and to wrest the government from him. Guglielmo de' Pazzi was commissary in the Val de Chiano in the year 1501. Having heard that a conspiracy had been organized in Arezzo in favor of the Vitelli, for the purpose of taking that place from the Florentines, he immediately went there, and without considering the strength of the conspirators or measuring his own, and wholly without any preparation, he had one of the conspirators seized by the advice of his son, the Bishop of Arezzo. Hereupon the others immediately took to arms, declared the independence of Arezzo, and made Guglielmo prisoner.

But when conspiracies are feeble, they can and ought to be crushed as promptly as possible; in such case, however, the two instances we shall quote, and which are almost the direct opposites of each other, should not in any way be imitated. The one is that of the above-name Duke of Athens, who, to prove his confidence in the attachment of the Florentines to him, had the man who denounced the conspiracy to him put to death. The other is that of Dion of Syracuse, who by way of testing the fidelity of some one whom he suspected ordered Callippus, in whom he had entire confidence, to pretend to be conspiring against him. Both, however, ended badly; the first discouraged the accusers, and encouraged those who were disposed to conspire; and the other paved the way for his own destruction, and was, as it were, the chief of the conspiracy against himself, as was proved by experience, for Callippus, being able to conspire with impunity against Dion, plotted so well that he deprived him of his state and his life.

Whoever Desires Constant Success Must Change His Conduct with the Times

I HAVE often reflected that *the causes of the succeess or failure of men depend upon their manner of suiting their conduct to the times.*

Here Machiavelli indicates that his tactics would change with the times. The advice is valid for the executive today. Long-term success depends upon altering one's behavior—one's strategies and tactics—to conform to the times. Big, free-wheeling gamblers do well in boom times but go down in flames in hard times; the conservative, close-to-the-vest businessman is jeered until recessions prove him competent. Rare is the man who can change with the times, so ingrained are his habits. What works for him once must work again—or so it seems to the unperceptive administrator.

In recent times, we have seen how corporate management has had to change its policies toward both the consumer movement and environmental considerations. Student unrest in the last few years has produced a different type of educational administrator. Those college presidents who were unable to adjust to the changing times were ruined.

We see one man proceed in his actions with passion and impetuosity; and as in both the one and the other case men are apt to exceed the proper limits, not being able always to observe the just middle course, they are apt to err in both. But he errs least and will be most favored by fortune who suits his proceedings to the times, as I have said above, and always follows the impulses of his nature. Everyone knows how Fabius Maximus conducted the war against Hannibal with extreme caution and circumspection, and with an utter absence of all impetuosity or Roman audacity. It was his good fortune that this mode of proceeding accorded perfectly with the times and circumstances. For Hannibal had arrived in Rome whilst still young and with his fortunes fresh; he had already twice routed the Romans, so that the republic was as it were deprived of her best troops and greatly discouraged by her reverses. Rome could not therefore have been more favored by fortune than to have a commander who, by his extreme caution and the slowness of his movements, kept the enemy at bay. At the same time, Fabius could not have found circumstances more favorable for his character and genius, to which fact he was indebted for his success and glory. And that this mode of proceeding was the result of his character and nature, and not a matter of choice, was shown on the occasion when Scipio wanted to take the same troops to Africa for the purpose of promptly terminating the war. Fabius most earnestly opposed this, like a man incapable of breaking from his accustomed ways and habits; so that, if he had been master, Hannibal would have remained in Italy, because Fabius failed to perceive that the times were changed. But Rome was a republic that produced citizens of various characters and dispositions, such as Fabius, who was excellent at the time when it was desirable to protract the war, and Scipio, when it became necessary to terminate it. It is this which assures to republics greater vitality and more enduring success than monarchies have; for the diversity of the genius of her citizens enables the republic better to accommodate herself to the changes of the times than can be done by a prince. For any man accustomed to a certain mode of proceeding will never change it, as we have said, and consequently when time and circumstances change, so that his ways are no longer in harmony with them, he must of necessity succumb. Pietro Soderini was in all his actions governed by humanity and patience. He and his country prospered so long as the times favored this mode of proceeding; but when afterwards circumstances arose that demanded a course of conduct the opposite to that of patience and humanity, he was unfit for the occasion, and his own and his country's ruin were the consequence. Pope Julius II acted throughout the whole period of his pontificate with the impetuosity and passion natural to his character; and as the times and circumstances well accorded with this, he was successful in all his undertakings. But if the times had changed so that different counsels would have been required, he would unquestionably have been ruined, for he could not have changed his character or mode of action.

That we cannot thus change at will is due to two causes: the one is the impossibility of resisting the natural bent of our characters; and the other is the difficulty of persuading ourselves, after having been accustomed to success by a certain mode of proceeding, that any other can succeed as well.

Military men frequently encounter difficulties in transferring their administrative talents to civilian tasks, for many of the tactics they used so successfully for 20 or 30 years simply don't work in industry. Conversely, "Engine" Charlie Wilson, who rose to head General Motors by using very strong, straightforward tactics, continually got into hot water employing the same tactics when he was Secretary of Defense.

This characteristic of man also hinders his advancement in management. The behavior that leads to success as a foreman may not be successful in the board room. The ambitious executive must perceive the behavioral changes required of him as he progresses up the ladder.

It is this that causes the varying success of a man; for the times change, but he does not change his mode of proceeding. The ruin of states is caused in like manner, as we have fully shown above, because they do not modify their institutions to suit the changes of the times. And such changes are more difficult and tardy in republics; for necessarily circumstances will occur that will unsettle the whole state, and when the change of proceeding of one man will not suffice for the occasion.

Whether an Able Commander with a Feeble Army, or a Good Army with an Incompetent Commander, Is Most to Be Relied Upon

CORIOLANUS, having been exiled from Rome, went to the Volscians, where he formed an army with which he returned to Rome to revenge himself upon his countrymen. But he soon withdrew again, influenced more by his affection for his mother than by the forces of the Romans. On this occasion, Titus Livius says: "It became evident that the Roman republic was more indebted for her aggrandizement to the merit of her generals than to that of their armies, seeing that the Volscians had until then always been defeated, and that they became victorious only when led by Coriolanus." And although Livius advances this

opinion, yet we find many instances in history where the
soldiers, deprived of their captains, have given wonderful
proofs of valor, and displayed more order and intrepidity
after the death of their Consuls than before. It was thus
with the army which the Romans had in Spain under the
Scipios, which, after the loss of both its commanders, not
only saved itself by its bravery, but actually defeated the
enemy and saved that province to the republic. So that on
the whole we shall find many instances of battles won solely
by the valor of the soldiers, and many others where the
same result was achieved by the courage of the general
alone. So that we may conclude that they are equally
dependent one upon the other.

It may be well here to consider which of the two is most
to be feared, a good army badly commanded, or a good
commander with a bad army. According to the judgment of
Caesar, neither one nor the other is worth much; for when
he went into Spain against Afranius and Petreius, who had
a good army under their orders, he said that he cared little
about that, "as he was marching against an army without a
chief," meaning thereby the weakness of the commanders.
And, on the other hand, when he went into Thessaly
against Pompey, he said "that he was marching against a
leader without an army." We may consider here also
another matter, namely, whether it be easier for a good
captain to form a good army, or for a good army to form a
good captain. Upon this point, I say that the question
would seem to be decided, inasmuch as it is much easier for
the many who have merit to find or instruct one to be
equally good, than for the one to form the many. Lucullus
was wholly inexperienced in war when he was sent against
Mithridates; nevertheless, being placed at the head of a
good army that had already very superior officers, he soon
became a good commander. The Romans, being in want of

men, armed a number of slaves and gave them to Sempronius Gracchus to be trained, who in a brief time made a good army of them. After Pelopidas and Epaminondas had delivered their country, Thebes, from the yoke of the Spartans, they made in a very short time the best kind of soldiers out of the Theban peasants; so that they were not only able to sustain the shock of the Spartan troops, but actually to defeat them. Thus the matter is about even; for if either one of the two, the army or the commander, be good, they will be apt to make the other good likewise. But a good army without an able commander often becomes insolent and dangerous, as was the case with the Macedonian army after the death of Alexander, and with the veteran troops in the civil wars of Rome. And therefore I am disposed to believe that *you can more safely rely upon a competent general, who has the time to instruct his men and the facilities for arming them, than upon an insolent army with a chief tumultuously chosen by them.*

Niccolò placed his money on management. Good management can develop good workers. Good workers can seldom shape up a poor management.

George Allen quickly altered the fortunes of the Los Angeles Rams and the Washington Redskins, in turn, upon assuming command—proof of the power of a great leader to turn the tide of affairs. Conversely, many teams loaded with talent have faltered under poor management. Note the fate of the Los Angeles Lakers—a team with a great talent, but hampered in its quest for greatness until Bill Sharman took over. Although it is admittedly too early to pass judgment on Sharman's reign, it is obvious at the time of this writing that he is getting far more effort and results from his stars than previous coaches.

It is also amazing how one able man can reverse the fortunes of a business that seems hopelessly headed for bankruptcy. American Motors' ill fortunes reversed suddenly when Chapin took the reins. A good man seems to attract other good men; he is not alone in the organization for long.

Those generals, therefore, deserve double praise and glory who not only had to conquer, but had actually to form and train their troops before meeting the enemy. For in this they have shown that twofold merit the union of which is so rare that many commanders, if they had been obliged to perform the same task, would not have obtained that celebrity which they have achieved.

Of the Effect of New Stratagems and Unexpected Cries in the Midst of Battle

WE HAVE numerous instances of the important effect produced by some unforeseen incident caused by something new that is seen or heard in the midst of a conflict or heat of battle. One of the most striking examples of this occurred in the battle between the Romans and the Volscians, when Quintius saw one wing of his army give way, and cried out to them in a loud voice to stand firm, as the other wing was victorious. These words reanimated the courage of his soldiers, and caused dismay amongst those of the enemy, so that Quintius carried off the victory. And if such a cry can produce such an effect in a well-disciplined

251

army, its influence is infinitely greater upon a tumultuous
and undisciplined body, who are all moved by similar
impulses. I will adduce a notable example of this, which
occurred in our own times. A few years ago the city of
Perugia was divided into two factions, the Oddi and the
Baglioni. The latter held the government and had exiled
the former, who, with the aid of their friends, gathered an
army, and established themselves at a convenient place
near Perugia. One night they entered the city by the aid of
their partisans, and, without being perceived, succeeded
in making themselves masters of the public square. As the
streets were all barred with chains, they had a man precede
them with an iron club to break the fastenings of these
chains, so that horses might be able to pass. Only one more
that closed the public square remained to be broken, and
already the cry of "To arms!" had been raised in the city.
Closely pressed by those that followed him, the man who
was charged to break the chains, unable to raise his arms
for the purpose, called out to those pressing upon him to
fall back. This cry of "Fall back!" taken up from rank to
rank, caused the hindmost to fly; the others, one by one,
followed them with such a rush that it ended in a complete
rout. And thus by this slight accident the whole project of
the Oddi was thwarted. This shows the necessity of discipline in an army, not only to make them combat with order,
but also to prevent any slight accident from creating confusion. And it is just for this reason that an undisciplined
multitude is useless in war; for the least unexpected noise
or word will throw them into confusion, and make them
take to flight. And a good commander should therefore,
amongst his other regulations, specially appoint persons to
receive his orders and transmit them to the others; and he
should accustom his soldiers not to listen to any but their
regular officer, and direct the officers to give no orders but

such as emanate from the commander. The nonobservance
of this rule has often caused the greatest misfortunes.

*As to new stratagems, when the armies are engaged in
conflict, every captain should endeavor to invent such as
will encourage his own troops and dishearten those of the
enemy.*

> The modern management trend toward a rather
> inflexible "game plan" for a venture would receive
> scant support from Niccolò, who saw considerable
> virtue in spontaneity in the course of affairs.
>
> One football coach learned Machiavelli's truth the
> hard way. In his early years, he formulated a game
> plan on Sunday for the following Saturday and stuck to
> it to the letter. No adjustments! Incredible! He couldn't
> understand why he lost the big ones. He was out-
> coached at every turn, but that was not the way he saw
> it. The quarterback club heard repeatedly, "We stuck
> to our game plan, but we weren't good enough to win."
> Baloney! It never occurred to this coach that his
> predictable adherence to a plan was the cause of his
> team's downfall. In time, he bent a bit, but not much
> —just enough to let his team win a few more games.
>
> How many firms get into hot water by following their
> game plans too exactly? "We will be highly
> leveraged"—and they are, regardless of the cost of
> funds and what could be earned on them. In theory,
> one should alter tactics and even strategies as de-
> velopments indicate or as opportunities present them-
> selves.

This is one of the most efficacious means of achieving
victory. In proof of which I will cite the example of the
Roman Dictator C. Sulpicius, who, being about to come to

battle with the Gauls, armed all the teamsters and camp-
followers, and mounted them upon the mules and other
beasts of burden, and supplied them with standards, so as
to seem like regular cavalry. These he placed behind a hill,
with orders to show themselves to the enemy at a given
signal during the heat of battle. This artifice, being carried
out as ordered, so alarmed the Gauls as to cause them to
lose the day. A good general, then, has to do two things: the
one, to try by novel strategems to create alarm amongst the
enemy; and the other, to be on his guard to discover those
that the enemy may attempt to practise upon him, and to
render them fruitless. It was thus that the Indian king
acted against Semiramis. This queen, seeing that the king
had a great many elephants, tried to frighten him by showing him that she had quite as many. She therefore ordered
a number of sham elephants made of the hides of buffaloes
and cows, which she had placed upon camels and sent to
the front. But the strategem was discovered by the king,
and proved, not only useless, but damaging to Semiramis.
The Dictator Mamercus was carrying on the war against
the Fidenati. These, for the purpose of frightening the
Roman army, caused, in the midst of an action, a number of
soldiers to issue forth from the city with burning torches at
the end of their lances, hoping that the Roman soldiers,
struck by the novelty of the thing, might break their ranks
and thus create confusion. Here it is well to observe that
such artifices may safely and with advantage be employed
when they have more the appearance of reality than of
fiction; for then their seeming strength will prevent the
prompt discovery of their weakness. But when they are
manifestly rather fictitious than real, they should either not
be employed, or they should be kept at such a distance that
their real character cannot be so quickly discovered, as
Sulpicius did with his muleteers. Otherwise, when too

near, their real weakness will be quickly discovered, and then they do more harm than good, as was the case with the sham elephants of Semiramis, and the torches of the Fidenati. For although these did at the first moment somewhat disturb the Roman soldiers, yet when the Dictator discovered it he called out to them to be ashamed to fly from the smoke like insects. "Return to the combat," he shouted to them, "and with their own torches burn their city of Fidena, which your benefits could not placate." Thus was the artifice of the Fidenati rendered futile, and the battle won by the Romans.

An Army Should Have But One Chief: A Greater Number Is Detrimental

THE FIDENATI, having revolted, massacred the colony which the Romans had established at Fidena. To avenge this outrage the Romans appointed four Tribunes with consular powers, one of whom remained to guard Rome, while the other three were sent against the Fidenati and Veientes. These three Tribunes gained nothing but dishonor in this expedition, in consequence of the dissensions that had arisen between them. For this dishonor they were themselves alone responsible; and it was only the valor of their soldiers that saved them from experiencing a serious check. The Romans, having perceived the cause of this

disorder, resorted to the creation of a Dictator; so that one
man might restore that order which the three Tribunes had
destroyed. Thence we may see the uselessness of several
commanders in one army, or in a city that is besieged. And
Titus Livius could not more forcibly illustrate this than
when he says: "Three Tribunes with consular powers
proved how useless it is to confide the command of an army
to several chiefs; for each one holding opinions of his own,
which the others would not adopt, they afforded the enemy
the opportunity to take advantage of their dissensions."
And although this example proves sufficiently the disad-
vantages resulting from a plurality of commanders for an
army in time of war, yet by way of still further elucidating
this truth, I will cite one or two other instances of both
ancient and modern times. When Louis XII, king of
France, had retaken Milan in the year 1500, he sent his
troops to Pisa, with orders to restore that city to the Florentines; whereupon the govenment of Florence sent there as
commissioners Giovanbattista Ridolfi and Luca d' Antonio
degli Albizzi. As Giovanbattista enjoyed a great reputation, and was the older of the two, Luca left the entire
management of affairs to him; and although he did not
exhibit his ambition by opposing him yet he manifested it
by his silence and by the indifference and contempt with
which he treated everything that was done, so that, neither
aiding in the actions in the field nor in council, one would
have supposed him to be a man destitute of all ability. But
he soon proved the very opposite, when, in consequence of
something that had occurred, Giovanbattista was obliged
to return to Florence. Then Luca, remaining in sole command, displayed his worth by his great valor, skill, and
wisdom, all of which were lost so long as he had a colleague
who shared in the command. I will quote once more, in
confirmation of what I have advanced, the authority of

Titus Livius. This historian, referring to the circumstance that the Romans had sent Quintius and Agrippa against the Equeans, adds, that the latter begged his colleague to take upon himself the sole conduct of the war, saying to him, "*In important affairs it is necessary for success that the principal authority should reside in one man only.*" This is just the contrary of what is done by our princes and republics of the present day, who confide to several commissaries and chiefs the administration of places subject to them, which creates an inconceivable confusion. And if we seek for the causes of the reverses experienced by the Italian and French armies in our times, we shall find that to have been the most powerful of all the causes. *So that we may truly conclude that it is better to confide any expedition to a single man of ordinary ability, rather than to two, even though they are men of the highest merit and both having equal authority.*

Something that is everyone's responsibility is no one's responsibility. Certainly the concept of fixing the responsibility for something that must be done on one person is a key principle of management. Yet we now hear about the "office-of-the-president" concept in which several men share the same position.

Is it any wonder that educational institutions are so ineptly managed? The places are largely run by committees.

In Times of Difficulty Men of Merit Are Sought After, But in Easy Times It Is Not Men of Merit, But Such as Have Riches and Powerful Relations, That are Most in Favor

IT EVER *has been, and ever will be the case, that men of rare and extraordinary merit are neglected by republics in times of peace and tranquillity; for jealous of the reputation which such men have acquired by their virtues, there are always in such times many other citizens, who want to be, not only their equals, but their superiors.*

The widely varying fortunes of Sir Winston Churchill provide one illustration of this aspect of human affairs. Let us delve into this facet of human frailty for a bit, because it is one of the barriers that conspires to keep

261

men of merit from their most useful roles in society.

In a very real sense, we are all in competition with each other for position, resources, and favor. Thus, men of merit pose a threat in all ways to men of lesser talents. Unfortunately, by the sheer weight of numbers, the mediocre manage to occupy all sorts of positions in society. From these, they form an effective, implicit conspiracy to prevent men of greater merit from assuming positions of power that will in any possible way prove threatening to them.

Moreover, mediocre men correctly surmise that their talents will not be evaluated favorably if men of ability become their superiors. The threat is very real. Consequently, talented men must disguise their abilities somewhat to gain the acceptance of their mediocre superiors and peers. Thus we can again see the wisdom of Machiavelli's previous advice that at times it is wise to "feign folly."

The Greek historian Thucydides gives the following striking instance of this. The Athenian republic, having obtained the advantage in the Peloponnesian war, having checked the pride of the Spartans and subjected almost all Greece to their rule, acquired such reputation that she conceived the project of conquering Sicily. This enterprise was much debated in Athens, Alcibiades and some other citizens, thinking more of the honor they could gain by it than of the public good, were much in favor of it, and hoped that the direction of it would be intrusted to them. But Nicias, one of the most influential citizens of Athens, opposed it, and the principal reason which he adduced against it, when addressing the people (who had faith in him), was this: that in advising them against this war he counselled them to what was against his own interest, for he well knew that so long as Athens remained at peace there were many citizens who wanted to take precedence of him; but he also knew that there was not a citizen who would pretend to show himself his superior, or even his equal, in time of war—thus showing that it is the common fault of republics in tranquil times to make small account of men of merit. And it is a twofold cause of indignation for such men to see themselves deprived of the rank to which they are entitled, and to be associated with, and often even subordinated to unworthy men, who are their inferiors in capacity. This defect in republics has often caused great evils; for those citizens who feel themselves so unjustly depreciated, and knowing it to be the result of the peace and tranquillity which the state enjoys, will stir up troubles and kindle fresh wars to the detriment of the republic.

In reflecting upon the means for remedying this evil, I believe I have found two. The first is to keep the citizens poor so that their wealth and lack of virtue may neither corrupt themselves nor enable them to corrupt others; and the second, so to organize for war as to be ever prepared for it, and always to have need of men of merit and reputation, as Rome did in her early days. For as this city always kept armies in the field, there was constant opportunity for the employment of men of ability; nor could rank be withheld from a man who deserved it, neither could it be bestowed upon another who did not merit it. And if, notwithstanding this, it was at times done, either by mistake or by way of trial, it caused at once such disorders and dangers that they quickly returned to the regular course. But other republics, which are not constituted like Rome, and who engage in war only when compelled by necessity, cannot avoid this inconvenience, but are rather constantly led into it. And this will always produce evil consequences whenever the meritorious citizen, who has thus been neglected, is disposed to be vindictive and has influence and partisans in the city. Rome avoided this evil practice for a time; but after she had conquered Carthage and Antiochus (as we have said elsewhere), and no longer fearing other wars, she also seems to have confided the conduct of her armies indifferently to whoever aspired to it, looking less to the merits and ability of the man than to such other qualifications as assured him favor with the people. For we see that the consulate was several times refused to Paulus Aemilius, and that he obtained it only when the war with the Macedonians occurred, which being deemed perilous, the command of the army was by general consent committed to him.

When after the year 1490 the city of Florence was involved in many wars, and her citizens had given but indifferent proof of their ability, the city by chance found a man who showed himself capable of commanding her armies. This was Antonio Giacomini; and so long as Florence had difficult wars on hand, all the ambition of her citizens ceased, and Antonio had no competitors for the part of commissary and chief of the army. But when there was a war that presented no dangers, and promised only honors and credit, then there were so many applicants that, in the appointment of three commissaries for the conduct of the siege of Pisa, Antonio was left out. And although the injury that resulted to the state from not having sent Antonio was not evident to all, yet it could most easily be conjectured. For Pisa, being destitute of munitions and provisions, would quickly have been forced to surrender at discretion to the Florentines, if Antonio had been in command. But the siege, being conducted by wholly incompetent men, was protracted to that degree that the Florentines had to resort to the purchase of the city, which they might otherwise have taken by force. Such an indignity might well have had an effect upon Antonio, and he must have been very good and forbearing not to have desired to revenge himself for it, either by the ruin of the state (which he could have occasioned) or by the destruction of some of his particular rivals. A republic should guard against similar dangers, as we will show more fully in the following chapter.

A Person Who Has Been Offended Should Not Be Intrusted with an Important Administration and Government

A REPUBLIC *should take great care not to intrust with an important administration one who has been gravely offended.*

Another warning along the lines of advice previously offered, but the problem may lie in knowing when you have offended someone, for you may be unaware of doing so.

Conversely, you should never gravely offend someone who holds an important office under you unless

267

you plan to remove him from office. The president of a medium-sized, family-controlled manufacturing concern had a very able sales manager whose advancement was blocked because of family considerations. The manager had an opportunity to get a much better job with a competitor, but the president stabbed him in the back by lying about the sales manager's character when asked for information about him. The competitor turned the sales manager down, but only after telling him why. The manager was furious; he kept his poise outwardly but extracted his revenge quietly over a period of several years. Not only were his expense accounts rather high, but he also managed to set up a competing company and throw some business its way before he was discovered.

Claudius Nero, who left the army with which he was confronting Hannibal and taking a portion of the same, went with it into La Marca to meet the other Consul, in order to engage Asdrubal before he could form a junction with Hannibal, found himself in front of Asdrubal and surrounded him with his forces in a place where he had to fight at a disavantage or die of starvation; but he was so craftily entertained by Asdrubal with propositions of an agreement, as to enable him to make his escape and defeat Nero's opportunity of crushing him. This becoming known in Rome, the Senate and people deemed it a grievous blunder, making him the constant topic of conversation about the city, to his great disgrace and shame. But afterwards becoming Consul and being sent against Hannibal, he acted in the manner above indicated, which involved such great danger that all Rome was troubled and in doubt until the news came of Asdrubal's rout. Claudius, being subsequently interrogated as to the reasons for taking so dangerous a course, by which without extreme necessity he had jeoparded the liberty of Rome, answered that he did so knowing that if successful he should regain the glory lost in Spain; and if unsuccessful, and his plan should have an adverse issue he would be revenged on that city and those citizens who had so ungratefully and indiscreetly offended him. And if such an affront could rouse to such passion a citizen of Rome in those days when Rome was yet incorrupt, we can imagine what might be done by a citizen of a city in a condition unlike that of Rome at that time. Hence, no adequate remedies existing for similar disorders arising in republics, it follows that it is impossible to estab-lish a perpetual republic, because in a thousand un-foreseen ways its ruin may be accomplished.

How States
Are Ruined on Account
of Women

Now how could I leave this out? Women's Lib, are you reading?

A difference arose in the city of Ardea between the patricians and plebeians on account of a rich heiress, who had been demanded in marriage by a plebeian and a noble at the same time. The young woman, having lost her father, her guardians wanted to give her to the plebeian, but the mother preferred the noble. This gave rise to such disturbances that they actually came to arms; the entire nobility armed in support of the young noble, and all the people in favor of the plebeian. The latter, having been overcome, left Ardea and sent to the Volscians for assistance, whilst the nobles applied to Rome. The Volscians, having arrived first, surrounded and besieged Ardea. When the Romans came, they shut in the Volscians between their army and the walls of the town, and pressed them so hard that, constrained by want of provisions, the Volscians were obliged to surrender at discretion. When the Romans entered the city, they put to death all the chiefs of the sedition, and reestablished order. This occurrence suggests several points for reflection; first, we see that women have been the cause of great dissensions and much ruin to states, and have caused great damage to those who govern them. We have seen, in the history of Rome, that the outrage committed upon Lucretia deprived the Tarquins of their throne, and the attempt upon Virginia caused the Decemvirs the loss of their authority. Thus, Aristotle mentions as one of the first causes of the ruin of tyrants the outrages committed by them upon the wives and daughter of others, either by violence or seduction; and we have discussed this subject at length when treating of conspiracies. I say, therefore, that absolute princes and rulers of republics should not be indifferent to this subject, but should well reflect upon the disorders that may arise from such causes, and should see that proper remedies be applied in time, ere they involve their state or republic in loss and shame. This happened to the people of Ardea, who, after having permitted the quarrel amongst their citizens (which we have mentioned above) to grow to that degree that it led to civil war, were obliged afterwards, by way of restoring union, to ask the intervention of strangers, which is a great step to a loss of independence.

The Faults of the People Spring from the Faults of Their Rulers

Let not princes complain of the faults committed by the people subjected to their authority, for they result entirely from their own negligence or bad example.

It was an industry convention. The sales managers were playing the "look at how lousy my men are" game. One expert in the field replied, "Who hired 'em? Who trained 'em? Who's lousy?" A man who complains about his subordinates should "take the Fifth" instead, for with each word he indicts himself.

In examining the people who in our day have been given to brigandage and other vices of that kind, we see that these arise entirely from the faults of their rulers, who were guilty of similar abuses. Before Pope Alexander VI had crushed the petty tyrants that ruled the Romagna, that country presented an example of all the worst crimes. The slightest causes gave rise to murder and every species of rapine; and this was due exclusively to the wickedness of the princes, and not to the evil nature of the people, as alleged by the former. For these princes, being poor, yet wishing to live in luxury like the rich, were obliged to resort to every variety of robbery. And amongst other dishonest means which they employed was the making of laws prohibiting some one thing or another; and immediately after, they were themselves the first to encourage their nonobservance, leaving such transgressions unpunished until a great number of persons had been guilty of it, and then suddenly they turned to prosecute the transgressors; not from any zeal for the law, but solely from cupidity, in the expectation of obtaining money for commuting the punishment. These infamous proceedings caused many evils; the worst of them was that the people became impoverished without being corrected, and that then the stronger amongst them endeavored to make good their losses by plundering the weaker. This gave rise to all the evils of which we have spoken above, and which are chargeable exclusively upon the princes. Titus Livius confirms this assertion when he relates how the Roman ambassadors, who were charged with carrying to Delphos a portion of the spoils taken at Veii and consecrated to Apollo, were captured by the corsairs of Lipari in Sicily, and carried on shore. The Prince Timasitheus, on being informed what gifts these ambassadors were carrying and their destination, conducted himself like a Roman, although a native of Lipari. He pointed out to his people how impious it would be to seize such a gift, and with the general consent allowed the ambassadors to depart with all their things. Upon which the historian remarks in the following terms: "Timasitheus inspired the multitude with a sentiment of religion, and they always imitate their rulers." And Lorenzo de' Medici confirms this idea by saying: "The example of the prince is followed by the masses, who keep their eyes always turned upon their chief."

To Insure Victory the Troops Must Have Confidence in Themselves as Well as in Their Commander

To MAKE *an army victorious in battle, it is necessary to inspire them with confidence, so as to make them believe that the victory will be theirs under any circumstances.*

Coaches call it pride; generals call it *esprit de corps*. Whatever term you care to use, organizations that have it fare better than one would expect; organizations without it fail to realize their potentialities. And Machiavelli tells you how to succeed: Be well armed and disciplined. Give your people good products, good

277

equipment, and good training. Encourage them to get to know one another. It's difficult to have much team spirit if you don't know the other members of the team.

And what destroys confidence?—Unconstructive criticism, nagging, uncertainty of leadership, business defeats, lack of personal success.

I was first exposed to the negative side of this managerial principle by a coach, better left unnamed, for whom no one could do right. To hear him tell it, his players were all worthless bums whose ineptness messed up each play. He screamed obscenities at them endlessly. Success was not to be found playing for him. And he never understood why his team lost, even expected to lose—or perhaps wanted to lose to punish their tormentor.

Fortunately, I was also privileged to observe closely the tactics of two great coaches and the impact they had on their players: Dr. Forrest ("Phog") Allen, the legendary University of Kansas basketball coach, and Bud Wilkinson, the University of Oklahoma football coach. There was never the slightest doubt in the minds of their players that victory would not be theirs. They knew they were the greatest. Their coaches had told them so and had proved it to them time and again.

Such confidence is not easily achieved. Many factors combine to create it. You begin by selecting men who not only want to win but who are accustomed to it. It is difficult to convince someone who has been losing that he can win. Winning is a habit. So is losing. Look for people with the habits you want.

But it is much easier to destroy confidence than it is to build it. Daily managerial tactics must constantly reinforce confidence. Both Coach Allen and Coach Wilkinson were magnificient confidence builders. One third-string bench warmer related, "I've gone to see Coach Wilkinson three times to tell him I was quitting—that I wasn't good enough to play football for him. Each time I came out of his office singing 'Boomer Sooner,' confident I could make a contribution to the team."

One of Oklahoma University's All-Americans once explained to me why the team would almost always be behind at halftime in difficult games but would come on strong in the third quarter to sweep the day. He said, "We don't worry about it. We know that Coach Wilkinson will tell us what we have to do to win. Then we go out and do it. We win!"

The wise manager strives for success. Once his people are conditioned to the fact that he provides success, they should accept his leadership unquestioningly.

But to give an army such confidence they must be *well armed and disciplined,* and the men must know each other; such confidence and discipline, however, can exist only where the troops are natives of the same country, and have lived together for some time. It is necessary also that they should esteem their general, and have confidence in his ability; and this will not fail to be the case when they see him orderly, watchful, and courageous, and that he maintains the dignity of his rank by a proper reputation. All this he will do by punishing faults, by not fatiguing his troops unnecessarily, by strictly fulfilling his promises, by showing them that victory is easy, and by concealing or making light of the dangers which he discerns from afar. These maxims well observed are the best means of inspiring the troops with that confidence which is the surest pledge of victory. The Romans were in the habit of resorting to religion for the purpose of inspiring their armies with confidence; and availed of auspices and auguries in the creation of their consuls, in the levying of troops, and before sending their armies into the field or engaging in battle. Without this no prudent captain would ever have hazarded an action, fearful of defeat if his soldiers had not been assured beforehand that they would have the gods on their side. And any consul or general who would have dared to combat contrary to the auspices would have been punished, as was done in the case of Claudius Pulcher. And although we find evidences of this practise throughout the history of Rome, yet we have still more conclusive proof of it in the words which Titus Livius puts into the mouth of Appius Claudius, who, complaining to the people of the insolence of their Tribunes, points out how by their means the auguries and other religious observances had been neglected and corrupted, saying: "It pleases them now to deride these religious practices, for they care not whether the fowls eat, or whether they come slowly out of their cages, or whether a bird sings; these are trifles for them; but such small matters are not to be contemned, for it was by their strict observance that our ancestors made this republic great." In fact it is little things of this kind that keep the soldiers united and confident, and these are essential elements of victory; though without courage they avail nothing.

The Praenestines, having taken the field against the Romans, took up a position on the river Allia, where the Romans had been defeated by the Gauls; hoping that the memories of that locality would inspire their own soldiers with confidence and discourage the Romans. Although the probabilities were in favor of this for the reasons above given, yet the event showed that true courage is not affected by such trifling incidents. Our historian expresses this thought extremely well by the words which he puts into the mouth of the Dictator in speaking to his master of cavalry:"You see the enemy, trusting to fortune, has chosen his position on the Allia; you, trusting to the arms and valor of your men, attack the very centre of their line of battle." For real courage, good discipline, and confidence founded upon so many victories cannot be extinguished by matters of such slight moment; nor can a vain idea inspire men animated by such feelings with fear, or a momentary disorder seriously injure them. This was clearly proven in the war against the Volscians, where there were two Consuls, both named Manlius. Having imprudently sent a part of their army to pillage the country, it happened that those who had been thus sent and those who remained in camp were both surrounded by the enemy at the same time; and from this danger they were delivered by their own valor and not by the prudence of the Consuls. Whereupon Titus Livius says, "The army, even without a chief, was saved by its own indomitable valor." I will not omit mentioning here an expedient employed by Fabius the first time he led his army into Tuscany. Wishing to inspire them with confidence, which he felt to be the more necessary as they were in a country entirely new to them, and opposed to an enemy whom they had not met before, he addressed his troops before going into battle; and after giving them many reasons for anticipating victory, he said "that he could give them other good reasons that would make their victory certain, but that it would be dangerous to reveal them at that moment." This artifice so judiciously employed well deserves to be imitated.

Of the Danger of Being Prominent in Counselling Any Enterprise, and How That Danger Increases with the Importance of Such Enterprise

IT IS too lengthy and important a matter to attempt here to discuss the danger of becoming the chief promoter of any new enterprise that affects the interests of the many, and the difficulties of directing and bringing it to a successful conclusion, and then to maintain it. Leaving such a discussion, therefore, till a more convenient occasion, I shall speak here only of those dangers to which those expose themselves who counsel a republic or a prince to undertake some grave and important enterprise in such a manner as to take upon themselves all the responsibility of the same. For as men only judge of matters by the result, all the blame of failure is charged upon him who first advised it; whilst in case of success he receives commendations, but *the reward never equals the punishment.*

A fact of life: Your boss will take the bows; you, the blows. You must give long and serious consideration to the wisdom of proposing some venture or program—no matter how good it may be—for its failure may be due to others, but you will reap the blame.

A new director of research at an educational institution proposed a program for assisting the business community in finding the information it needed. While his boss had voiced a desire for working with business, he did nothing to support the director's idea, so it never got off the ground. The director quietly dropped his plans for the program. Thereafter, the dean turned that incident against the director as an example of how he "didn't follow through on his ideas."

The present Sultan Selim, called the Grand Turk, having prepared (according to the report of some who have come from that country) to make war upon Syria and Egypt, was advised by one of his Pashas, who was stationed on the borders of Persia, rather to march against the Shah. Influenced by this advice, the Sultan started upon that enterprise with a very powerful army. Having arrived in that country, where there are vast deserts and little water, he experienced all the same difficulties that had in ancient times caused the loss of several Roman armies there. These difficulties were so overwhelming, that, although always successful against the enemy, yet he saw a large part of his army destroyed by pestilence and famine. This so infuriated the Sultan against the Pasha who had advised this enterprise that he put him to death. History relates many instances of citizens having been sent into exile for having counselled enterprises that terminated unsuccessfully. Some Roman citizens were foremost in urging the selection of Consuls from amongst the people. It happened that the first one so chosen was defeated with his army in the field, and the originators of that system would certainly have been punished if the party to conciliate which it was adopted had not been so powerful.

Thus be warned that the sponsor of an idea assumes great responsibility: He may be unjustly blamed for its results and most likely will reap few rewards for its authorship. Is it any wonder that bureaucracies are so sterile of ideas and new ventures?

Certainly those who counsel princes and republics are placed between two dangers. If they do not advise what seems to them for the good of the republic or the prince, regardless of the consequences to themselves, then they fail of their duty; and if they do advise it, then it is at the risk of their position and their lives; for all men are blind in this, that *they judge of good or evil counsels only by the result.*

It matters not how well you play, but whether or not you win the game. Sorry, Grantland, you were full of . . . wishful thinking.

In reflecting as to the means for avoiding this dilemma of either disgrace or danger, *I see no other course than to take*

*things moderately, and not to undertake to advocate any
enterprise with too much zeal, but to give one's advice
calmly and modestly.*

This passage saved one man from making a serious
blunder. A small cog in a huge organization full of an
unbelievable amount of bureaucratic red tape, he had
been made responsible for a small operation. He had
grandiose plans to "really do something for a change."
As time passed and organizational inertia affected his
resolution, he drastically scaled down his plans (after
reading this passage). He is now nicely ensconced in
the organization's bureaucratic quagmire and is well
thought of for foregoing the perils of a bold venture.

If then either the republic or the prince decides to follow
it, they may do so, as it were, of their own will, and not as
though they were drawn into it by your importunity. In
adopting this course it is not reasonable to suppose that
either prince or republic will manifest any ill will towards
you on account of a resolution not taken contrary to the
wishes of the many. For the danger arises when your
advice has caused the many to be contravened. In that
case, when the result is unfortunate, they all concur in your
destruction. And although by following the course which I
advise you may fail to obtain that glory which is acquired by
having been one against many in counselling an enterprise
which success has justified, yet this is compensated for by
two advantages. The first is, that you avoid all danger; and
the second consists in the great credit which you will have
if, after having modestly advised a certain course your
counsel is rejected, and the adoption of a different course
results unfortunately. And although you cannot enjoy the

glory acquired by the misfortunes of your republic or your prince, yet it must be held to be of some account.

I do not believe that I can give a better advice upon this point than the above; for to advise men to be silent and to withhold the expression of any opinion would render them useless to a republic, as well as to a prince, without avoiding danger. For after a while they would become suspect, and might even experience the same fate as that which befell a certain friend of King Perseus of Macedon. This king having been defeated by Paulus Aemilius and having fled with a few adherents, it happened that, in discussing the late events, one of them began to point out to Perseus the many errors he had committed, to which he ascribed his ruin. "Traitor," exclaimed the king, in turning upon him, "you have waited until now to tell me all this, when there is no longer any time to remedy it"—and with these words he slew him with his own hands. Thus was this man punished for having been silent when he should have spoken, and for having spoken when he should have been silent: His having withheld his counsel from the king did not save him from danger. I believe, therefore, that it is best to adopt the course I have advised above.

Any Manifest Error on the Part of an Enemy Should Make Us Suspect Some Strategem

FULVIUS, HAVING been left as lieutenant of the Roman army in Tuscany whilst the Consul had gone to assist at some religious ceremonies, the Tuscans attempted to draw him into an ambush which they had placed near the Roman camp. For this purpose they sent some soldiers, disguised as herdsmen, with a drove of cattle, who approached the intrenchments within sight of the Romans. The lieutenant wondering at their presumption, which did not seem reasonable to him, suspected and discovered the deceit, and thus defeated the design of the Tuscans. *This instance will serve to show that the commander of an army should*

289

always mistrust any manifest error which he sees the enemy commit as it invariably conceals some stratagem. For it is not reasonable to suppose that men will be so incautious.

> Three men were engaged in various businesses to-gether. Two of the men did some things that seemed totally stupid to the third man. Finally, after several months, the third man realized that the other two were in the process of swindling him out of $250,000. And they succeeded, for the third partner did not fathom their motives soon enough. He could have squelched their plans if he had protected himself when they made their first "stupid" move.
>
> Men always have reasons for what they do. The fact that you do not understand them only means that you lack some critical information. When you do not understand something, look for hidden motives—look for the financial interests.

But the desire of victory often blinds men to that degree that they see nothing but what seems favorable to their object. After their victory over the Romans on the Allia, the Gauls marched upon Rome, and, finding the gates open and unguarded, they remained a whole day and night without entering, fearing some stratagem, and unable to believe that the Romans were so cowardly and so ill-advised as to abandon their city. When the Florentines, in 1508, went to besiege Pisa, Alfonso del Mutolo, a citizen of that town, who had fallen into their hands, promised, if they would grant him his liberty, to deliver to them one of the gates of Pisa. His offer was accepted, and he was set free. Afterwards he came several times to confer on the subject with the deputies of the commissaries, but never concealed his visits, coming openly and accompanied by several Pisans, whom he left apart whilst conferring with the Florentines. From this circumstance, his duplicity might readily have been conjectured; for it was not reasonable that he should have treated a matter of this kind so openly if he had been acting in good faith. But the eager desire to possess Pisa so blinded the Florentines that, under his guidance, they advanced to the gate of Lucca, where, by the double treason of the said Alfonso, they lost in a discreditable manner a number of their officers and men.

ATE DUE